OECD Reviews of Risk Management Policies

Trends in Risk Communication Policies and Practices

This work is published under the responsibility of the Secretary-General of the OECD. The opinions expressed and arguments employed herein do not necessarily reflect the official views of OECD member countries.

This document and any map included herein are without prejudice to the status of or sovereignty over any territory, to the delimitation of international frontiers and boundaries and to the name of any territory, city or area.

Please cite this publication as:
OECD (2016), *Trends in Risk Communication Policies and Practices*, OECD Reviews of Risk Management Policies, OECD Publishing, Paris.
http://dx.doi.org/10.1787/9789264260467-en

ISBN 978-92-64-26040-5 (print)
ISBN 978-92-64-26046-7 (PDF)

Series: OECD Reviews of Risk Management Policies
ISSN 1993-4092 (print)
ISSN 1993-4106 (online)

The statistical data for Israel are supplied by and under the responsibility of the relevant Israeli authorities. The use of such data by the OECD is without prejudice to the status of the Golan Heights, East Jerusalem and Israeli settlements in the West Bank under the terms of international law.

Photo credits: Cover Illustration © Jeffrey Fisher.

Corrigenda to OECD publications may be found on line at: *www.oecd.org/about/publishing/corrigenda.htm*.

Foreword

Governments have a key responsibility in communicating to citizens about the risks that confront them. Citizens expect to be notified about known perils and impending threats. They also expect governments to provide guidance on what protective actions to take. Raising awareness about the risks of high-impact, low-probability events represents a particular challenge; these events happen just rarely enough that most citizens forget about them, or think that they only happen to other people.

This study was undertaken to assess countries' progress in putting in place effective risk communication policies and practices, as spelled out in EU guidance documents and the OECD Council Recommendation on the Governance of Critical Risks, adopted in 2014. The study relies upon a unique country survey that captures for the first time a comprehensive set of information on progress in risk communication practices as well as country perspectives on the challenges they confront. The 19 country responses show that significant progress has been made by governments to make risk communication effective in reducing exposure to, and impacts from, disasters. For example, governments are taking responsibility for communicating about risks at national level while working collaboratively across levels of government to tailor their communication to different groups and localities. The survey finds high recognition among government authorities of the need to involve the private sector whose activities can have an important impact on risks. Despite significant achievements, countries still face constraints to improve the effectiveness of their risk communication. Top-down approaches, which involve one-way communication from the government to society, have impeded higher levels of risk awareness. Countries have been slow in adopting two-way communication tools to make risk communication more inclusive. The wealth of experiences gained from past risk communication efforts could be exploited to design more effective actions for the future. Even though two-thirds of countries surveyed evaluated the impact of their risk communication policies, the results are rarely reported and the lessons learned hardly ever used to change policy practices.

This study was undertaken by the OECD, in cooperation with the European Commission, precisely to address these challenges, and to map progress in risk communication practices. It was undertaken under the aegis of the OECD High Level Risk Forum, which brings together policy makers from governments, practitioners from the private sector, and experts from think tanks and academia to identify and share good practices and deepen their understanding of risk management.

ACKNOWLEDGEMENTS

This report was prepared by the OECD Public Governance and Territorial Development Directorate, led by Rolf Alter (Director) and Luiz de Mello (Deputy Director). It was co-ordinated by Catherine Gamper. Charles Baubion and Catherine Gamper co-wrote Chapter 1. Chapter 2 and 3 were written by Catherine Gamper. Guidance and supervision were provided by Stéphane Jacobzone, Deputy Head of the Reform of the Public Sector Division, and Jack Radisch, Senior Project Manager. Roberto Schiano Lomoriello provided valuable research assistance and significant substantive contributions.

This report has benefitted from the financial and substantive support of the European Commission's Directorate General for Humanitarian Aid and Civil Protection (DG ECHO).

The Secretariat would like to thank participants at the OECD High Level Risk Forum in 2014 and 2015, where the general policy evaluation framework was initially presented and the survey results were subsequently discussed. Particular thanks go to the experts of 19 countries who provided informative results to the OECD survey on Risk Communication Policies and Practices. A preliminary version of this report was also presented at the EU Working Party on Civil Protection (PROCIV) in May 2016 and the Secretariat would like to also thank participants for the informative discussions.

Marie-Claude Gohier and Lynda Hawe prepared this report for publication. Kate Lancaster and Andrea Uhrhammer offered valuable editorial comments.

Table of contents

Tables

Figures

Boxes

Acronyms

BRIC	Brazil, Russia, India and China
COBR	Cabinet Office Briefing Room (United Kingdom)
DHS	Department of Homeland Security (United States)
DICRIM	Document d'information communal sur les risques majeurs (France)
DG ECHO	Directorate General For Humanitarian Aid and Civil Protection
EU	European Union
ERA	European Research Area
FEMA	Federal Emergency Management Agency (United States)
GDP	Gross Domestic Product
GIS	Geographic information systems
ICT	Information and communication technology
MRN	Mission Risques Naturels (France)
NGO	Non-governmental organisation
PROCIV	Working Party on Civil Protection (DG ECHO)
SAGE	Scientific Advisory Group in Emergencies (United Kingdom)

Executive summary

During the past 10 years, OECD countries and Brazil, Russia, India and China (the BRIC countries) have experienced an estimated USD 1.5 trillion cost from economic damages caused by natural disasters such as storms or floods, or by man-made disasters such as industrial accidents or terrorist attacks. Individual events like the 2010 earthquakes in New Zealand and Chile caused damages in excess of 20% of their national GDPs.

A sound risk management strategy seeks to reduce future human and economic losses and damage from disasters. Risk communication is a fundamental part of such a strategy. Effective risk communication increases the awareness of the stakeholders, such as households, businesses and communities about their exposure and vulnerability to hazards. It also informs them about measures they themselves can take for prevention, mitigation and emergency preparedness. Furthermore, spreading the knowledge of risk exposure can spur an informed debate about the need for public investment to prevent, mitigate and prepare for disasters.

Without good risk communication, the public may underestimate some risks, and thus take insufficient precautions, and overestimate others, leading to sub-optimal allocation of resources. Governments have a basic responsibility to notify citizens about their exposure to major hazards and threats. However, effective risk communication needs to be inclusive, engaging public actors from all levels of government, as well as private actors from companies, civil society organisations and citizens.

For this report, a survey was carried out to systematically assess countries' progress in setting up effective risk communication policies and practices, as spelled out in EU and OECD policy guidance documents. The survey responses from 19 countries captures, for the first time, a comprehensive set of information on governments' risk communication activities and the perspectives of the underlying challenges.

Risk communication is improving…

- Communication about risks is a widely shared, cross-governmental responsibility. In the 19 countries that responded to the survey, national governments led risk communication, but they did so in close co-operation with subnational governments. In many countries, national authorities provide guidance and technical assistance on risk communication to the other levels of government.
- Risk communication matters for crisis situations, and governments have established solid crisis communication policies and practices based on risk monitoring and early warning systems.
- Most OECD countries have recognised the need to adapt risk communication to the needs of different audiences. To save children's lives and to build risk awareness from an early age, risk communication is now part of school curricula. Other vulnerable groups, such as the elderly or disabled people, have also been given specific attention. For example, in Turkey, a mobile phone application informs visually impaired people about earthquake alerts.

… but challenges persist

- There is a significant divergence between how experts understand risks and how the public perceives them. The results of a survey among 1 700 companies, from the Loire River basin in France, showed that over half of business owners whose activities were located in flood zones were unaware of their exposure. Following the 2007 floods in the United Kingdom, a study highlighted that 84% of affected residents believed there was nothing they could do to protect their homes, with half of respondents firmly believing that it is not their responsibility to invest in making their homes safer.
- The longer the time has passed since a major disaster event, the harder it is to keep risk awareness levels high, since memories fade.
- Traditional crisis communication has been particularly one-sided, delivering messages in a top-down fashion.
- Adapting governments' risk communication practices to rapidly changing risk environments has proved to be challenging.

Key policy recommendations

- **Governments' risk communication needs to become more inclusive**, involving citizens and other stakeholders actively in a two-way communication process and building partnerships with the private sector. This to ensure that risk information is well received and that it can be improved in line with citizens' needs. It will also help citizens develop a shared understanding of risks and to maintain trust in their government's ability to manage risks.
- **Risk communication should be grounded in up-to-date scientific evidence** to ensure quality and accuracy. This can also help promote new risk communication tools for a more comprehensive and, ultimately, effective, risk communication.
- **Countries need to exploit new technology, including social media.** Risk communication is characterised by uncertainty, by rapid changes and developments; it thus requires flexible communication tools and channels. Countries could use modern technology more effectively to issue warnings and interact about ongoing crises with the affected people. Two-way communication via interactive media also allows citizens to provide feedback that can help improve future risk communication policies and practices.
- **Countries need to focus more on prevention,** informing stakeholders about what they can do to help reduce their risk exposure. Responding countries have all developed tools to communicate the potential risks in different parts of their countries. Often, this information is conveyed through easily accessible and easy-to-use tools, where individual stakeholders can view their exact location's exposure to risk. However, this is not enough. Countries also need to communicate about actions individual stakeholders can take to reduce their risk exposure.

Chapter 1

Risk communication: Theory, policy and practice

This chapter introduces the concept and objectives of effective risk communication. It distinguishes between the traditional focus of emergency or crisis communication and the more comprehensive risk communication approach, which uses risk communication before an event to strengthen prevention and mitigation efforts. While a significant amount of evaluations have been done on the effectiveness of crisis communication, much less work has been carried out on the use of risk communication to strengthen risk prevention and mitigation. The chapter provides an overview of the two policy frameworks this report is based on, the EU Council Conclusions on an Integrated Approach to more Effective Risk, Emergency and Crisis Communication and the OECD Recommendation on the Governance of Critical Risks. Finally, it presents the risk communication framework established to inform the design of an OECD survey instrument to assess countries' risk communication policies and practices.

Introduction

In the last decade, OECD countries and Brazil, Russia, India and China (the BRIC countries) have experienced an estimated USD 1.5 trillion in economic damage from disruptive disasters – both natural disasters such as storms or floods, and man-made ones such as industrial accidents or terrorist attacks. Individual disasters, such as the 2010 earthquakes in New Zealand and Chile, have caused damage in excess of 20% of national gross domestic product (GDP), and particularly affected local economies and populations. Not only are disasters occurring more frequently in recent decades but, perhaps more importantly, they have significantly increased in intensity and complexity. Among the factors driving this surge in intensity is the increased concentration of people – especially elderly, more vulnerable people – and economic assets in risk-prone areas. Urbanisation has reinforced and accelerated this dynamic. Increased global economic integration, facilitated by transport mobility and communication, has helped to propagate shocks globally. Deteriorating environmental conditions coupled with climatic changes have equally contributed to these trends. The failure of one country to identify and manage a major risk can have tremendous negative impacts on others.

Risk communication is a fundamental element of a sound risk management framework that seeks to reduce future losses and damages from disasters. Governments have a basic responsibility to engage with all actors in society to notify them about their exposure to major hazards. Effective risk communication increases the awareness of households, businesses and communities about their exposure to risk and their vulnerabilities, and also informs them what specific prevention, mitigation and preparation measures they could take. Such knowledge can also spur an informed debate on the need for public investment in prevention, mitigation and preparedness, and is thus a key element of good governance in risk management policy.

Ineffective risk communication can lead the public either to underestimate risks, which may result in them taking insufficient precautionary measures, or to overestimate them, leading to sub-optimal allocation of resources. Despite concerted government actions to raise and maintain awareness of hazards and threats, there can be a significant divergence between experts' understanding of risks and the general public's perception of risks. For example, a survey of 1700 companies in the Loire River basin in France found that 53% of the business owners whose activities were located in a flood zone admitted to being completely unaware of their exposure (OECD, 2010a). Following the 2007 floods in the United Kingdom, a study highlighted that 84% of affected residents believed there is nothing they can do to better protect their homes in the future, with half of respondents firmly believing that it is not their responsibility to invest in making their homes safer (Pitt, 2008). Areas with low levels of awareness about existing hazards and whose responsibility it is to take protective measures lead to endemic low levels of resilience, i.e. the capacity of an area to regain function promptly after a disruption.

Few countries find that their risk communication efforts fully achieve their desired objectives, yet many of them continue to use the same techniques that have failed in the past, in the hope that the target audience will pay more attention this time. Therefore it makes sense to identify novel and effective risk communication practices across OECD countries to inform countries' risk communication developments in the future.

This publication presents the results of a comparative analysis of risk communication policies and practices across OECD countries. It includes the results of an OECD survey of 19 countries that was developed and carried out in 2015. The survey builds on a framework, which was developed from policy recommendations put forward in the OECD Recommendation on the Governance of Critical Risks (OECD, 2014a) and the EU Council Conclusions on an Integrated Approach to more Effective Risk, Emergency and Crisis Communication (EU, 2011). This chapter outlines the rationale and importance of risk communication within the overall risk management process as well as the elements of good risk communication policy design. It presents a risk communication policy framework that includes a comprehensive set of elements that should be part of a good risk communication policy mix. The policy framework builds the basis for the development of a survey instrument that is used to gather information on the progress of implementing risk communication policies into practice across OECD and some of its partner countries. Chapter 2 presents the results of the OECD survey of risk communication policies and practices. Chapter 3 summarises policy recommendations and discusses options for taking this work forward.

Defining risk communication and its functions

Risk communication needs to be distinguished from emergency and crisis communication. Risk communication needs to be done before a hazardous event occurs, to inform citizens and businesses about their potential exposure and to encourage them to invest in precautionary measures to avoid, reduce or transfer these risks. In contrast, emergency and crisis communication needs to inform people once the event is imminent, has already begun or has just occurred. Risk communication then comes to the fore again in the aftermath of disasters, to make sense of what happened, to learn lessons, to improve risk management and ultimately to strengthen trust among all actors for risk management.

While linkages between risk, emergency and crisis communication exist, there are significant differences in scope, objective, timing and surrounding circumstances between the two. This study focuses on risk communication, but will also explore any relevant linkages with crisis and emergency communication with a view to achieving an integrated approach.

Risk communication seeks to fulfil different functions, each of which requires different policy designs. The set of risk communication functions is well summarised in the definition of risk communication by the US Department of Homeland Security (DHS):

"Risk communication is the exchange of information with the goal of maintaining or improving risk understanding, affecting risk perception and/or equipping people or groups to act appropriately in response to an identified risk" (US DHS, 2008).

Similarly, the OECD (2002) sets out four core objectives of risk communication which are 1) education and enlightenment; 2) risk training and inducement of behavioural changes; 3) confidence in institutions' ability to manage risks and 4) inclusion of stakeholders in risk management decisions. Box 1.1 describes these objectives in more detail.

The US DHS and the OECD definitions of risk communication both underline the need to not simply inform recipients but to change their behaviour, to make all actors take on responsibility for actively reducing risks.

Box 1.1 The purpose and function of risk communication

The OECD (2002) distinguishes four major functions of risk communication:

1. **Education and enlightenment**: to inform about risks and the handling of these risks.

   This function is a complicated and challenging process because it needs to take into account a society's perception of risk. Risk research has shown that the basic understanding of risks differs within societies, making risk communication even more important for effective and efficient risk management, because it helps improve the public's understanding of risks. Successful risk communication needs first a common understanding of the term risk and, second, common moral understanding, experiences and values with a common set of signs and symbols (Hampel, 2006). In this sense, effective risk communication needs to provide an adequate understanding of the known facts, including what can be perceived as uncertain and ambiguous.

Box 1.1 The purpose and function of risk communication *(continued)*

2. **Risk training and inducement of behavioural changes**: to help people to cope with risks.

   This function assists people in changing their daily behaviour or habits to reduce their risks to life and personal health. Sunstein (2005) argues that emotions lead to various errors in risk perception, among which is the failure to appreciate probabilities. To change the risk perceptions and behavioural responses of recipients in the desired ways, risk communicators need to design several programmes with the purpose of raising awareness about risk and "nudging" people's behaviour.

3. **Raising confidence in institutions of risk assessment and risk management**: to assure people that the existing governance structures are capable of handling risk in an effective, efficient, fair and acceptable manner.

   Establishing and gaining the public's trust is key to effective risk management because, in a society that trusts the messages delivered, risk communication can mitigate negative risk perceptions. Trust grows with the experience of trustworthiness; therefore, trust needs to be developed over time (Renn, 2010). In an empirical study, Peters et al. (1997) identified three determinants of trust and credibility in the context of environmental risk communication: 1) the perception of knowledge and expertise; 2) the perception of openness and honesty; and 3) the perceptions of concern and care. All three aspects need to be taken into account for a successful and effective communication.

4. **Involvement in risk-related decisions and conflict resolution**: to give stakeholders and representatives of the public the opportunity to participate in risk assessment and to be included in conflict resolution about risks.

   The main purpose of involving stakeholders and the public in the risk assessment and management process is to improve the quality of decision making and also to avoid damaging and time-consuming confrontations. However, the intensity and scope of stakeholders' involvement depends on the issue and the extent of the controversy (Renn, 2010). Risk communication needs to take this into account when letting different stakeholders participate in risk assessment.

Sources: OECD (2002), *Guidance Document on Risk Communication for Chemical Risk Management*, www.oecd.org/officialdocuments/publicdisplaydocumentpdf/?doclanguage=en&cote=env/jm/mono(2002)18; Hampel (2006), "Different concepts of risk – A challenge for risk communication"; Peters et al. (1997), "The determinants of trust and credibility in environmental risk communication: An empirical study"; Renn (2010), " Risk communication: Insights and requirements for designing successful communication programs on health and environmental hazards"; Sunstein (2005), *Laws of Fear: Beyond the Precautionary Principle.*

The OECD work also emphasises a crucial additional function, which is the importance of risk communication to ensure trust in government and its institutions. Trust in government is particularly tested during disastrous events, and is generally lower in many countries following crises. As a result, governments in many countries have been forced to take drastic actions to restore trust. If previous neglect or lack of action to reduce risks becomes apparent during a major shock, this often has a disproportionately negative effect on trust in government. For example, the Great East Japan Earthquake raised serious concerns among citizens about whether the government did enough to foresee and protect citizens against the cascading impacts of a large earthquake on nuclear power stations. The earthquake in L'Aquila in Italy raised concerns among citizens about their level of risk awareness and on the lack of communication by the government on how to improve resilience (OECD, 2010b). Natural disasters are not the only events which have sparked such trust issues. Plane crashes, violent attacks and financial crises have raised similar doubts about governments' policies and engagement (OECD, 2014b).

Risk communication can be a key to maintaining and, where necessary, restoring trust in government after disastrous events. In many cases governments may have to react with drastic measures to restore trust among citizens after disastrous events. Senior leaders may be forced to resign and government officials or experts taken to court and given prison sentences for neglect, or been banned from practising their professions in the future. For example, in the United States, the director of the Federal Emergency Management Agency (FEMA) had to resign after the controversial handling of Hurricane Katrina in September 2005. However, in many of these cases no single person is to blame, and such drastic measures can be avoided if governments invested more in communicating their risk management efforts to citizens and other stakeholders more effectively (OECD, 2014b).

Effective risk communication enables stakeholders to manage risks more effectively, to negotiate who owns the risks, and to know what their role is in contributing to the different phases of the risk management cycle (Höppner et al., 2010). The first point of departure is to identify and assess existing hazards, threats and related vulnerabilities (Figure 1.1). Communicating the risks that have been identified and assessed is key to assisting stakeholders to understand the rationale behind such assessment results and risk management decisions, and to help them understand this information in the context of their own interests and values (OECD, 2003).

Figure 1.1 The role of risk communication in the risk management cycle

Source: adapted from Health Protection Network (2008), "Communicating with the public about health risks", www.documents.hps.scot.nhs.uk/about-hps/hpn/risk-communication.pdf.

Once risk communication has transmitted expert knowledge to the public, differences between public perceptions and expert judgement may come into play. This is why, in many countries, the one-way transfer of hazard and threat-related information and its management has given way to a more interactive, two-way exchange of related information, knowledge, attitudes and values. The interactive approach brings together the public, those stakeholders who are directly or indirectly affected, and risk managers to engage in a social learning process, to build mutual trust, and to communicate outcomes in an open and transparent manner (Leiss, 1996). The ultimate aim of good risk communication is to prevent crises, to inform policy decision processes and to make policy implementation smoother. It should also empower and reassure the public, and to help build trust in government and in the information it provides (Höppner et al., 2010).

The development of information and communication technology (ICT) has facilitated the use of social media for risk communication. Because social media is a decentralised communication tool, it helps transmit information repeatedly through different channels, increasing the chances of reaching those who need the information, and adapting risk communication to different target populations (Wendling et al., 2013). Social media can enable two-way risk communication by developing dialogues between different stakeholders in advance. However, social media can also create new risks, by spreading incorrect information about threats, undermining the efforts of official risk management and emergency preparedness authorities. Governments have a role to play in monitoring the accuracy of information flows by interacting with stakeholders to verify the trustworthiness of emerging information.

Many of these elements form part of a good policy mix for risk communication and have been enshrined in national legislation and also in international risk management recommendations. The next section considers the two most relevant international policy guidance instruments from the European Union and the OECD.

The role of risk communication in OECD and EU recommendations

Both the OECD and the European Union have issued policy recommendations on risk communication. The objective of this report is to integrate these recommendations into the policy evaluation framework and to assess progress in implementing these policy recommendations among OECD and partner countries.

EU Council Conclusions on an Integrated Approach to more Effective Risk, Emergency and Crisis Communication

The EU Council Conclusions on an Integrated Approach to more Effective Risk, Emergency and Crisis Communication (EU, 2011) emphasise the need for risk communication to enable citizens to recognise risks and take actions to reduce their potential exposure. The EU conclusions are in line with the OECD Recommendation on Governance of Critical Risks (OECD, 2014a) which recommends "a whole-of-society approach to risk communication and facilitate trans-boundary co-operation using risk registries, media and other public communications on critical risks". The OECD proposes two-way communication between governments and stakeholders, combining targeted communication with incentives and tools for stakeholders to invest in resilience measures.

The EU Council Conclusions emphasise the importance of risk communication for civil protection, with the goal of making citizens safer and more secure, by enabling them to recognise risks, to take precautionary measures to avoid risks, and to react swiftly to minimise risks, limiting the consequences of emergencies. The EU Council Conclusions rests upon several key points:

- The recognition of the importance of an integrated approach to risk, emergency and crisis communication, that entails interaction and co-ordination between risk management actors including: public authorities, international organisations, non-governmental organisations (NGOs), citizens, the media, businesses and citizens' associations, as well as trade unions at local, national and international levels.
- The need to provide warnings and alerts regarding actual or potential risks and threats and instructions on how to behave in such events, giving this information on a timely basis, transparently and consistently conveyed, and circulated in a proper and balanced way. Such information needs to be tailored to local conditions, and made accessible and understandable to people from other cultures (such as travellers) exposed to local threats.
- The recognition of new channels of information as an opportunity to improve risk communication by complementing conventional communication channels with modern technologies and interactive media (such as social media), although the local, linguistic cultural, social, economic, risk and technical conditions need to be taken into account when designing risk communication strategies. To promote these new risk communication tools, co-operation with scientific centres and the private sector are encouraged.
- The promotion of dialogue with the public and the increase of their knowledge on risk and emergency management systems, including risk communication, through education and training.

There are also practical, very concrete measures that need to be promoted to improve risk communication effectiveness. This includes raising the public's awareness of the European emergency call number "112" and making available sufficient radio spectrum for public safety, civil protection and disaster relief, ensuring that wireless communication systems operate effectively without harmful interference.

The EU Council Conclusions demonstrate that the objectives of risk communication can be diverse. Consequently risk communication practices may take several forms. A comprehensive risk communication policy should consider all of the following objectives:

- Informing the public about the different hazards and threats they may face and the related vulnerabilities.
- Facilitating collective choices by informing public debate and collective discussion about risk management policies.
- Educating the public about risk reduction and preparedness measures for specific emergencies by recommending precise and dedicated approaches.

The role of risk communication in the OECD Recommendation on the Governance of Critical Risks

The OECD High-Level Risk Forum promotes an all-hazard (natural and men-made hazards) and a whole-of-society approach to risk management. It recognises that individuals, businesses and governments from national to local levels should all take part in bearing the risks. The fundamental role of governance is thus to co-ordinate the roles and responsibilities among all these different actors across the whole risk management cycle.

This approach is developed in the OECD Recommendation on the Governance of Critical Risks (OECD, 2014a), which is designed to assist governments, policy makers and senior officials charged with developing and maintaining robust risk management frameworks and their implementation. The OECD proposes a set of policy recommendations based on the five pillars in Box 1.2.

Box 1.2 Overview of the OECD Recommendation on the Governance of Critical Risks

Pillar 1: Establish and promote a comprehensive, all-hazards and trans-boundary approach to country risk governance as the foundation for enhancing national resilience and responsiveness. This pillar focuses on the importance of framing risk management policies at a national scale through which all major risks are accounted for and designated to responsible agencies. National leadership should articulate clear goals and mobilise support for the priorities identified.

Box 1.2 Overview of the OECD Recommendation on the Governance of Critical Risks *(continued)*

Pillar 2: Build preparedness and identify critical hazards and threats, through foresight analysis, risk assessments and financing frameworks, to better anticipate complex and wide-ranging impacts. This pillar highlights the key capacities that should be developed to anticipate critical risks, monitor the quality of capabilities to deal with them, and provide the flexibility in public budgets to plan for unplanned impacts due to cataclysmic events.

Pillar 3: Raise awareness of critical risks to mobilise households, businesses and international stakeholders and foster investment in risk prevention and mitigation. The efficiency and effectiveness of risk governance is grounded in putting exposed populations on notice and providing the information they need to take protection measures. This pillar emphasises the importance of co-operation between countries and with other key actors, including the private sector, building common ground and promoting continuous improvements with regards to the governance and management of critical risks and ensuring stable and secure communities.

Pillar 4: Develop adaptive capacity in crisis management by co-ordinating resources across governments, its agencies and broader networks to support timely decision making, communication and emergency responses. Establishing strategic crisis management capacities is critical for governments to prepare for unexpected and novel risks that provoke crises. This pillar emphasises the need to strengthen crisis leadership, early detection and sense-making capacity, and conduct exercises to support inter-agency and international co-operation and to establish the competence and capabilities to scale up emergency response capacities. It also aims to close the policy cycle, through planning of recovery and rehabilitation efforts.

Pillar 5: Demonstrate transparency and accountability in risk-related decision making by incorporating good governance practices and continuously learning from experience. This pillar aims to ensure that risk-related decision making is subject to transparency and accountability and is supported by clear evidence-based processes and communication as a way to foster trust in government through good governance. It should help governments in conjunction with governmental and non-governmental organisations, to make trade-off decisions informed by the full country portfolio of critical risks, fostering the continuous sharing of knowledge and lessons learned.

Source: OECD (2014a), *Recommendation of the Council on the Governance of Critical Risks*, www.oecd.org/gov/risk/recommendation-on-governance-of-critical-risks.htm.

While Pillar 3 addresses risk communication explicitly (Box 1.3), all five pillars contain elements that are relevant for risk communication. Table 1.1 summarises these links.

Box 1.3 OECD guidance on raising awareness of exposure to risks and facilitating co-operation

Encourage a whole-of-society approach to risk communication and facilitate trans-boundary co-operation using risk registries, media and other public communications on critical risks through:

1. **two-way communication** between governments and stakeholders, ensuring that information sources are accurate and trusted, and the information is made accessible in a manner appropriate to diverse communities, sectors, industries and with international actors

2. the combination of **targeted communication** with the provision of incentives and tools for individuals, businesses and NGOs to work together and take responsibility for investment in self-protective and resilience-building measures

3. **providing notice** to households about different scales of hazards and human-induced threats, and supporting informed debate on the need for prevention, mitigation and preparation measures

4. **informing and educating the public** in advance of a specific emergency about what measures to take when it occurs, and mobilising public education systems to promote a culture of resilience by integrating community resilience skills and concepts into curriculums and thereby pass information on to households through students.

Source: OECD (2014a), *Recommendation of the Council on the Governance of Critical Risks*, www.oecd.org/gov/risk/recommendation-on-governance-of-critical-risks.htm.

Table 1.1 Linkages between the OECD Recommendation and risk communication

Pillar	Main focus	Key notions/ and potential linkages related to risk communication
1	Comprehensive approach to risk governance	• Risk communication as part of a national strategy for risk governance. • All-hazards and threats approach to risk communication. • Clear designation of responsibilities among institutions in risk communication, allowing a multidisciplinary and multi-agency approach. • Engagement of all actors within government, from national to local levels, and partnerships with the private sector (e.g. media).
2	Risk assessment	• Risk communication practices based on risk knowledge developed through risk assessment processes. • Regular update of risk communication practices and tools coinciding with advancements in risk knowledge. • Communicate the results of the National Risk Assessment to the public, in summary or in full.
3	Awareness & prevention	• Pillar 3 develops specifically the notion of risk communication - see Box 1.3 above.
4	Crisis management	• Awareness of emergency preparedness measures and early warning systems as part of risk communication policies and practices. • Synergies between risk communication and emergency/crisis communication (stakeholders, technical tools and platforms, and symbols).
5	Good governance	• Transparency on the risk information utilised by governments to take decisions. • Accountability linked to the risk information communicated to the public. • Evaluation of the effectiveness of risk communication policies.

Source: OECD (2014a), *Recommendation of the Council on the Governance of Critical Risks*, www.oecd.org/gov/risk/recommendation-on-governance-of-critical-risks.htm.

Pillar 3 sets out the criteria for effective risk communication:

- **Consistency**: it is fundamental to ensure that risk information is consistent across the different risk communication tools. Inconsistencies in this domain can lead to ineffective policies, lack of trust and inaction.

- **Two-way communication**: risk communication should not be seen as only transmitting expert knowledge to the public. More interactive approaches bring together the public with risk managers to engage in an exchange of risk information. Among other things, this allows stakeholders to be engaged more actively in risk reduction efforts, more and broader information to be gathered about risks and the efficiency of risk communication tools to be evaluated through feedback loops.

- **Accuracy and trust**: risk communication should be based on the best available knowledge on hazards, threats and vulnerabilities. Risk information should be fully transparent about the level of accuracy, to ensure that risk information is trusted and acted upon.

- **Accessibility**: while risk communication supposes dedicated and targeted actions, citizens and business should also be provided with easy-to-use and accessible risk information portals and repositories.

- **Adapted to the audience**: specific segments of society should be targeted by dedicated risk communication, from national to local levels, vulnerable groups, children and elderly, communities, and non-residents (such as tourists) in ways that are adapted to both their cognitive capacities and their specific exposure or vulnerabilities.

- **Cross-sectoral and trans-boundary**: risk communication should incorporate information from different sectors so that the public has a clear picture of the multiple dimensions of potential hazards and threats, and their potential cascading effects. Policy makers should also address the issue of consistent communication across regional and/or national borders, both for cross-border hazards and to ensure that investors, travellers, tourists and other stakeholders can understand risk information in other countries.

Both the EU and OECD policy guidance documents thus provide detailed recommendations for an effective policy mix for risk communication. Both include important elements that have been established in policy research on risk communication and that have been identified as good risk communication practices. For example, they recognise the different functions risk communication should fulfil, from informing recipients of risk communication messages to positively influencing their behaviour. Both policy documents recognise the importance of the mode of communication, emphasising the need to include citizens actively in the risk communication process and tapping into innovative technologies to channel messages and organise interactions more effectively.

The following section presents a policy framework setting out a comprehensive set of elements that should be included in a good policy mix for designing risk communication strategies.

A risk communication policy evaluation framework

The goal of this project is to evaluate progress in OECD and partner countries in implementing the risk communication policies proposed in the EU and OECD policy guidelines. To do this systematically across countries requires an operational policy evaluation framework that can subsequently be transformed into a country survey instrument that can be found in Annex A.

The draft framework presented in Table 1.2 follows the broad principles described in this chapter. It is also informed by a complementary review of recent academic literature so as to ensure the development of a comprehensive framework. The framework is built on seven overall pillars:

1. **Actors** include a list of actors in charge of communicating risks. It is important to understand how responsibilities are shared among them. This pillar is also critical to evaluating the implication of non-governmental actors in the risk communication process, especially the role of the private sector.
2. **Risk types** look at whether an all-hazard approach is used in communicating risks and to what extent risk communication strategies integrate notions of complexity and cascading effects.
3. **Purpose** seeks to evaluate the risk communication objectives. It assesses whether communication is focused on measures to prepare for emergency situations or whether it communicates actions that can prevent or mitigate impacts before a disaster.
4. **Modes and channels** identify how communication is delivered, for example whether risks are communicated only one way or whether it establishes two-way flows of information. It also looks at what types of channels are used for communicating, for example conventional (TV, radio) or modern communication technologies (social media).
5. **Tools**: these differ from communication channels in that they look at the means of communication, such as through the use of "quiet witnesses" or objects that indicate the physical extension of past hazardous events.
6. **Message**: the risk communication messages need to be honest about what risk managers know and do not know. The modes also include language, cultural and social aspects of communicating with different target audiences.

7. **Good governance arrangements** characterises to what extent risk communication policy is handled based on good governance principles, such as openness and transparency, inclusiveness and grounding in evidence. This pillar also evaluates the ability to incorporate lessons learned from previous risk communication practices into the design of new policies.

In the following table, a policy evaluation framework is presented that is informed by the EC and OECD policy recommendations on risk communication described above. The policy evaluation framework presented in Table 1.2 provides a description of each element of a country risk communication strategy, followed by a set of policy evaluation questions. These questions informed the design of the survey instrument presented in Annex 1 and carried out among OECD countries. The results of this survey are presented in Chapter 2.

Table 1.2 Proposed analytical framework for assessing risk communication practices

Pillar of risk communication	Description	Questions for assessment
Actors	National government Local government Elected officials at national and local levels Other public agencies International organisations Scientists and experts Industry, private sector Trade unions Critical infrastructure providers NGOs and voluntary organisations Exposed-affected public Local communities Vulnerable groups (including people with disabilities) General public Mass media	Who are the main actors with responsibility for risk communication? How are the responsibilities for communicating risks shared and organised among the key actors at local, regional and national level? What are the responsibilities of the private sector for risk communication? Do critical infrastructure providers have special responsibilities? How is communication organised in small settings, among individuals, groups and local communities? What are the key processes for exchanging information and communicating across major public and private institutions?
Risk types	Hazard-specific All-hazard approaches Complex risk	Is there an all-hazard and threat approach to risk communication or specific risk communication approaches pertaining to specific hazards? How are the notions of complexity and cascading effects conveyed in risk communication effectively?

Table 1.2 Proposed analytical framework for assessing risk communication practices *(continued)*

Pillar of risk communication	Description	Questions for assessment
Purposes	Raise public awareness about hazards and risks/enhance knowledge through education and training Encourage protective behaviour Information promoting the acceptance of risk management measures Inform on how to behave during hazardous events Warn of and trigger actions in response to imminent and current events Reassure the audience, improve relationships (build trust, co-operation and networks) Enable mutual dialogue and understanding Involve actors in decision making as a means to promote capacity development at the individual, group, community and organisational level	How is communication organised? Does it focus on the existing risks, and/ or the potential measures to prepare or prevent? What is the scope of communication? Is it limited to simply informing or does it engage in actions and in providing guidance? Is the communication aimed at improving confidence and trust? How is it organised to reach this goal and what are the results? How are actors involved in framing the communication and in the communication process? Is the risk communication accessible to vulnerable groups
Modes and channels	Written (newspaper, letter, reports) Verbal (lectures, storytelling, conversation) Non-verbal/visual (gestures, body language, sign language, facial expressions, graphics, movies) One-way or two-way Direct, (face-to-face through meetings, focus groups, lectures) or mediated/indirect (letters, reports, telephone, videoconferences or, for a larger audience, brochures, leaflets booklets mass media and social marketing) Conventional and interactive media (such as social media) Information networks	How is the communication delivered? Does the communication flow only one or two-ways? If it flows two-ways, how exactly does this take place? Is the chosen communication channel direct or indirect? Is it done through conventional and/or interactive media (such as social networks)? What are the barriers to the communication? What is the role of social media in the communication strategy and how is it mobilised?

Table 1.2 Proposed analytical framework for assessing risk communication practices *(continued)*

Pillar of risk communication	Description	Questions for assessment
Tools	"Quiet witnesses" (e.g. marking historical disaster events in a visible way) Objects that indicate the geographical extension of past hazardous events Information boards next to eye-catching structural measures Use of modern technologies, including satellite-based technologies and systems using geospatial information Use of digital content and tools Integrating behavioural science findings	What kinds of tools are used to communicate? What is the role for modern technologies, including mobile based content and apps? What is the role for behavioural science and psychological experiments? Are digital content and tools used? How are the tools organised to facilitate citizen-centred communication?
Message	Must be honest, comprehensive Should include what is known, but also unknown Language is understood differently by different stakeholders (such as 100 year return of flood) Language should motivate attitude and behaviour change, instead of provoking fear, stress, and powerlessness Consideration of the prevailing cultural, social, linguistic, risk economic and technical conditions Be accessible to different audiences and target groups, including vulnerable people (e.g. people with disabilities)	How are communication messages framed? Are communication messages adapted to different audiences, languages? How do they take account of prevailing conditions in various areas of the country? Are they accessible to the different audiences and target groups, including vulnerable groups (e.g. people with disabilities) What do the messages entail? Does it address trans-boundary risks?
Good governance	Openness and transparency Involvement (engagement in decision processes) Proportionality and consistency Evidence based Responsibility (allocating responsibility for risk management appropriately) Efficiency of information flow Integrated approach for risk, crisis and emergency communication	How is risk communication made open and transparent? Is it consistent and based on evidence? How efficient is the information flow? Are there any studies to assess the impact? Is there an integrated approach to risk, crisis and emergency communication?

Source: adapted from Höppner et al. (2010), *Risk Communication and Natural Hazards,* CapHaz-Net.

The OECD survey on risk communication policies and practices focuses on the identification of good risk communication policy and practice based on the framework outlined in Table 1.2. The instrument seeks first to understand the broader institutional context, which includes the responsibilities of governments and other stakeholders, including the private sector, in communicating risks. The survey then looks at whether risk communication is addressed primarily by hazard type or whether multiple risks are addressed simultaneously. The survey seeks to understand the modes and channels of communication, including whether and how recipients are included in the risk communication processes. Finally, the survey considers good governance arrangements, such as the way lessons have been learned from previous risk communication experiences and incorporated into current risk communication policy design.

The next chapter provides an overview of the results of this survey. It presents overall country responses and highlights good practice. The risk communication practice examples provided by countries were complemented by additional research, where necessary, so as to be able to provide an understanding of the wider country policy context. Chapter 3 provides a set of policy recommendations for improving risk communications and discusses options for taking this work forward.

Bibliography

EU (2011), "Council conclusions on an integrated approach to more effective risk, emergency, and crisis communication", 3135th Justice and Home Affairs Council Meeting, Council of the European Union, 13 and 14 December, Brussels, www.consilium.europa.eu/uedocs/cms_data/docs/pressdata/en/jha/126887.pdf.

Hampel, J. (2006), "Different concepts of risk – A challenge for risk communication", *International Journal of Medical Microbiology*, Vol. 296/Supplement 1, pp. 5-10.

Health Protection Network (2008), "Communicating with the public about health risks", *Health Protection Network Guidance*, Health Protection Scotland, www.documents.hps.scot.nhs.uk/about-hps/hpn/risk-communication.pdf.

Höppner, C., M. Bründl and M. Buchecker (2010), *Risk Communication and Natural Hazards*, CapHaz-Net WP5 Report, CapHaz-Net, Birmensdorf, Switzerland.

Leiss, W. (1996), "Three phases in the evolution of risk communication practice", *The Annals of the American Academy of Political and Social Science*, Vol. 545/1, pp.85-94.

OECD (2014a), *Recommendation of the Council on the Governance of Critical Risks*, OECD Publishing, Paris, www.oecd.org/gov/risk/recommendation-on-governance-of-critical-risks.htm.

OECD (2014b), *Boosting Resilience through Innovative Risk Governance*, OECD Publishing, Paris, http://dx.doi.org/10.1787/9789264209114-en.

OECD (2010a), *Étude de l'OCDE sur la gestion des risques d'inondation: Bassin de la Loire, France 2010*, OECD Publishing, Paris. http://dx.doi.org/10.1787/9789264056817-e

OECD (2010b), *OECD Reviews of Risk Management Policies: Italy 2010: Review of the Italian National Civil Protection System*, OECD Publishing, Paris, http://dx.doi.org/10.1787/9789264082205-en.

OECD (2003), *Emerging Risks in the 21st Century: An Agenda for Action*, OECD Publishing, Paris, http://dx.doi.org/10.1787/9789264101227-en.

OECD (2002), *Guidance Document on Risk Communication for Chemical Risk Management*, ENV/JM/MONO(2002)18, Joint Meeting of the Chemicals Committee and the Working Party on Chemicals, Pesticides and Biotechnology, OECD, Paris, www.oecd.org/officialdocuments/publicdisplaydocumentpdf/?doclanguage=en&cote=env/jm/mono(2002)18.

Peters, R.G., V.T. Covello and D.B. McCallum (1997), "The determinants of trust and credibility in environmental risk communication: An empirical study", *Risk Analysis*, Vol.17/1, pp. 43-54.

Pitt, M. (2008), "The Pitt Review: Learning Lessons from the 2007 Floods", UK Cabinet Office, London.

Renn, O. (2010), "Risk communication: Insights and requirements for designing successful communication programs on health and environmental hazards", in H. Dan O'Hair & Robert L. Heath (eds.), *Handbook of Risk and Crisis Communication*, Routledge.

Sunstein, C.R. (2005), *Laws of Fear: Beyond the Precautionary Principle*, Cambridge University Press.

US DHS (2008), *Risk Steering Committee: DHS Risk Lexicon*, United States Department of Homeland Security, Washington, DC, www.dhs.gov/xlibrary/assets/dhs_risk_lexicon.pdf.

Wendling, C., J. Radisch and S. Jacobzone (2013), "The use of social media in risk and crisis communication", *OECD Working Papers on Public Governance*, No. 24, OECD Publishing, Paris, http://dx.doi.org/10.1787/5k3v01fskp9s-en.

Chapter 2

Comparing risk communication policies and practices across countries: Results from an OECD survey

This chapter provides an overview and a discussion of the results of a cross-country survey that was conducted on risk communication policies and practices. The survey sought to uncover the core elements of countries' risk communication strategies. This includes the general governance arrangements and the roles of actors responsible for risk communication. It also investigates countries' objectives in their risk communication efforts, looking at the tools they use to achieve them. The survey also looks at the policies and practices countries have in place to ensure quality and inclusiveness in their risk communication processes. This includes approaches countries have to evaluate the impacts of risk communication efforts and to incorporate lessons learned into future risk communication strategies. Good country practices are highlighted throughout the chapter.

Introduction

This chapter presents the results of the survey on risk communication policies and practices in OECD and partner countries. The full survey is included in Annex A. Based on the policy evaluation framework developed in Chapter 1, the survey was designed to uncover the key elements of countries' risk communication strategies, from general governance arrangements, to the type of risks that are covered and the arrangements in place to ensure quality, inclusiveness and impact evaluation (Figure 2.1). The survey seeks to give a comparative overview of risk communication policies and identify good practices to inform countries wishing to reinforce their current policy frameworks. The survey results also contribute to tracking countries' progress in implementing the policy recommendations developed by the EU and OECD described in the previous chapter.

Figure 2.1 Core elements of a country risk communication system

The results that follow are based on a response from 19 countries (Austria, Australia, Colombia, France, Germany, Greece, Japan, Korea, Luxembourg, Malta, Mexico, Norway, Poland, the Slovak Republic, Slovenia, Sweden, Switzerland, Turkey and the United Kingdom). Naturally, many answers only reflect the viewpoint of the institution responding to the survey, rather than the full array of risk communication activities carried out by all government agencies within a country. To inform the reader, Annex B provides the full list of responding countries and the name of the institution that answered to the survey.

General institutional arrangements and responsibilities for communicating about risks

Communicating about risks is a shared task. As Figure 2.2 shows, risk communication in all responding countries is overseen by national governments and shared with subnational level governments. This reflects the strategic nature of risk communication, which should be led by the national government, while at the same time be adapted to specific local exposures, which are best understood by subnational governments.

Figure 2.2 Actors with legal or formal responsibilities for risk communication

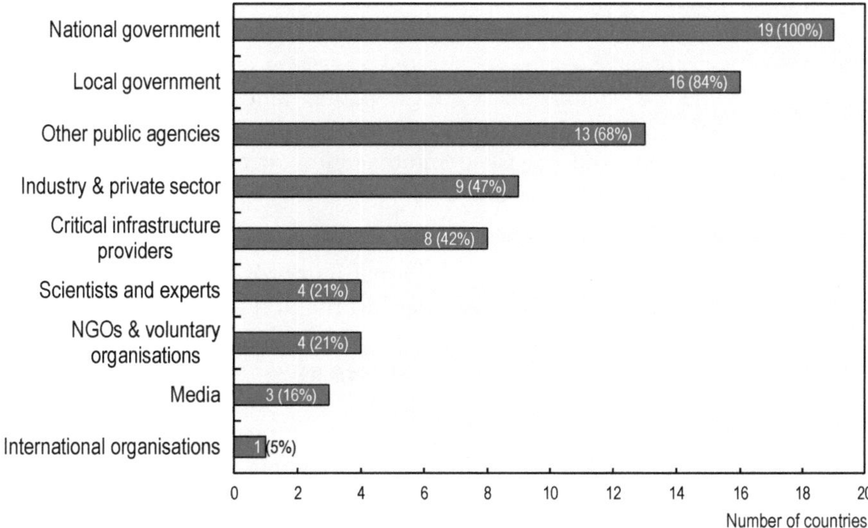

Note: Total number of responding countries: 19/19.

Source: OECD Questionnaire on Risk Communication Policies and Practices. Question 1.2 (Annex A).

Almost all responding countries confer responsibility for communication about specific risks onto a specific authority. With the exception of Austria, Germany, Poland and the Slovak Republic, all countries have lead organisations or co-ordinating platforms for risk communication, which might be a civil protection authority or other national authority in charge of disaster risk management. For example in Norway the Directorate for Civil Protection and Emergency Planning developed and operates a specific online platform to convey messages to citizens. The platform provides an online portal informing citizens about their individual vulnerability to both natural and man-made hazards as well as the measures they can take to become more resilient.[1] In Australia, Emergency Alert is a national online risk communication platform for emergency services.[2] Emergency Alert delivers messages as either text-to-voice for landlines, or texts to mobile phones. This emergency service reaches everyone with access to a telephone and network coverage anywhere in Australia, whether they are at home, travelling or an international visitor roaming into Australian mobile phone networks.

The private sector has an important role to play in supplying information for risk communication, but also communicating about risks itself. The private sector has to share information with public authorities especially when its activities pose a safety hazard to the wider public, such as industrial hazards or nuclear power accidents. The Seveso Directive of the European Commission formally establishes such a role in Europe.[3] This Directive suggests that communicating about risks stemming from private sector activity should be channelled through public authorities to inform the potentially affected population. The survey results show that the private sector has a formal role in risk communication in only about half of the responding countries (Figure 2.2).

To facilitate collaboration between the private sector and public authorities in communicating risks, information needs to be exchanged in an effective way. Channels for exchanging information about risks turn out to be diverse and can be formal, such as regular reports or meetings, or informal, such as the use of emails, text messages and phone calls (Figure 2.3). Formal exchanges are often well established when the activities of the private sector could pose threats to the public resulting from industrial activities dealing with hazardous materials. Spontaneous meetings are often called by public authorities on a needs basis, for example, when private sector organisations and companies can provide financial, technical or in-kind contributions for a more efficient risk communication. France has established partnerships and platforms for exchanges between public authorities and private sector actors that are often used to discuss risk communication strategies and to jointly train actors responsible for risk communication (Box 2.1). The Austrian Civil Protection Association, for instance, is a private organization with nine regional branches which informs the public about risks and self-protection measures (Box 2.2).

Figure 2.3 Channels for exchanging information about risks between the private sector and public authorities

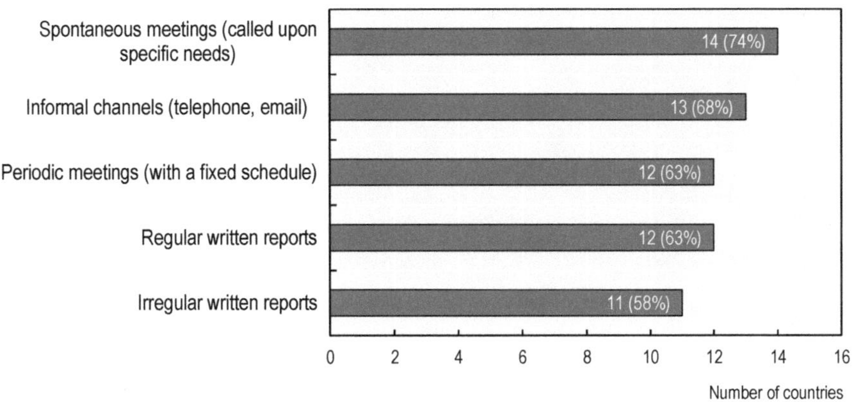

Note: Total number of responding countries: 19/19.

Source: OECD Questionnaire on Risk Communication Policies and Practices. Question 1.7 (Annex A).

Box 2.1 Good practice: France's Mission Risques Naturels (MRN): facilitating risk communication between the private and the public sectors

Mission Risques Naturels (MRN) is a French based association of two insurance societies which was created in 2000 after a year especially marked by catastrophic floods and storms in France. The MRN is the technical correspondent between the insurers and other public stakeholders engaged in natural risks management. The purpose of the association is for insurance professionals to contribute to a better understanding of natural hazards and make a technical contribution to prevention policies.

The MRN has three main pillars of work:

- acting as the technical interface between the insurance profession and the various public stakeholders in the management of natural hazards
- working on insurance-related prevention studies
- a focal point for gathering the risk-related concerns of insurance companies for the public authorities.

The MRN also publishes monographs on lessons learned from the occurrence of major natural hazards, as well as various reports and indicators.

Source: Mission Risques Naturels (2015), *Insurance and Climate Risks Prevention*, www.mrn.asso.fr/system/files/15%2010%2001%20Brochure%20Prevention%20VAng.pdf.

Box 2.2 Good practice: The Austrian Civil Protection Association: the private sector's risk communication on behalf of the Federal Ministry of the Interior

The Austrian Civil Protection Association is a collective comprising ten associations, one federal organisation and nine regional offices, whose task is to inform the population on civil defence in Austria, particularly on adequate behaviour in emergency situations. According to the association´s statutes of 1993, its mission is the following:

- to promote the idea of self-protection through events, presentations and the dissemination of information to the population
- to coordinate and collaborate with the regional offices
- to train and advise the population in matters of civil defence, collaboration with the responsible authorities and intervention organisations
- to prepare and assess proposals for the creation of regulations within the framework of civil protection
- to exchange experience with foreign civil protection organisations.

The association is, unlike the fire brigade and rescue organisation, not active on an operational level, but one whose main task is to disseminate risk-related information to the population. The association acts, in this matter, on behalf of the Federal Ministry of the Interior and forwards all information on self-protection to the public through two different channels:

- general public information on civil protection
- the organisation of safety and security information centres (SIZ) at a local community level.

Sources: Ministry of Interior, Austria (2016), Information on Austria's Civil Protection Agency, www.bmi.gv.at/cms/BMI_Zivilschutz_en/national/civil/start.aspx; Austrian Civil Protection Association, www.zivilschutzverband.at/home.

Approaches to risk communication

A comprehensive, all-hazards and trans-boundary approach to country risk management enhances national resilience and responsiveness. Such an approach allows countries to identify how risks and critical systems interrelate. This knowledge can then be integrated across sectoral policies and programmes and inform interagency approaches. An all-hazards approach also strengthens the development of a clear vision and shared strategy among all actors in society. The same principles apply to risk communication.

More than half of respondent countries have an all-hazards approach to communicating about risks (Figure 2.4.). For example, the General Secretariat for Civil Protection in Greece possesses cross-sectoral competence to take an all-hazards risk management approach in general, which is translated into their risk communication work,[4] including information about preparedness and prevention of natural as well as man-made hazards. Australia's all-hazards approach to general risk management is reflected in both state and territorial risk assessments and its respective communication strategies building on them. In the United Kingdom, the Cabinet Office draws together all key hazards and threats into a single, collective National Risk Register, which is a public resource for individuals and organisations to be better informed about and prepared for emergencies (Table 2.1).[5]

Table 2.1 National Risk Register in the United Kingdom

Practice	Communication from....	....to	General Objectives
The National Risk Register alerts the public to all types of events the government considers to be the highest actual risk to incite the public to take measures to increase its own resilience.	Central government Dedicated ministry Sectoral ministry National agency	Sectoral ministries Local governments Local communities Citizens Companies Non-governmental organisations (NGOs)	• Inform the public about natural and man-made risks • Increase awareness • Incentivise to take actions • Increase public trust in government • Facilitate and inform debate

Countries that do not take an all-hazards approach, in general have a different administrative risk management set-up with different types of risks being managed by different agencies, which makes it difficult to reconcile an all-hazards approach to risk communication with their separate mandates.

Figure 2.4 All-hazards or specific hazards approach to communicating risks

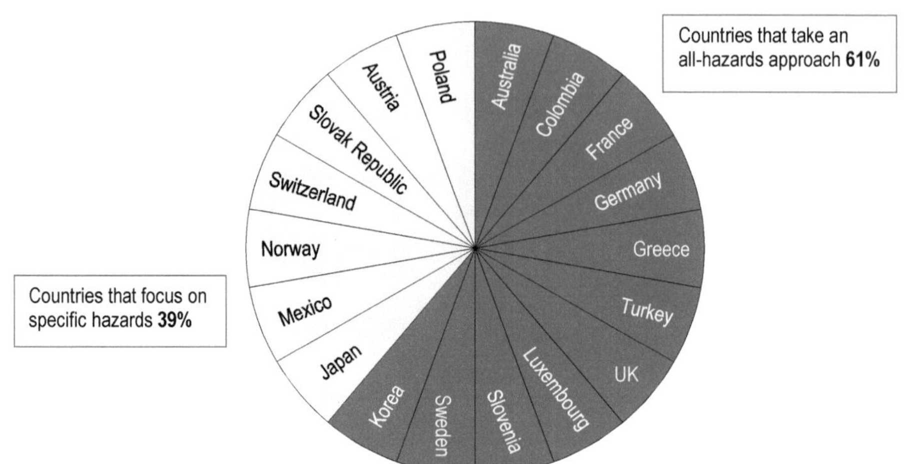

Note: Total number of responding countries: 18/19 (excluding the "don't know" replies).

Source: OECD Questionnaire on Risk Communication Policies and Practices. Question 2.1 (Annex A).

Apart from taking all hazards into account, a comprehensive approach to risk communication does not only look at past and present hazards as well as single occurring ones, but takes into account compounding and future potential hazards. Countries' risk communication strategies are not as forward looking, taking future risk patterns into account, as they could be, suggesting possible difficulties in identifying future risks or in communicating them. Although 71% of countries integrated notions of complex or cascading risks – such as an earthquake triggering a tsunami – into their risk communication strategies (Figure 2.5), about half stated that their risk communication strategies focused exclusively on known risks (Figure 2.6). Some countries have begun to integrate future and cascading hazard scenarios in their national risk assessments. For example, the United Kingdom addresses risks it has not yet experienced by considering cascading effects as both "linked risks" and "compound risks". In general, countries understand the importance of having a set of preparedness measures, especially in the event of mega-shocks that could trigger cascading effects.

Figure 2.5 Communicating about complexity and cascading effects

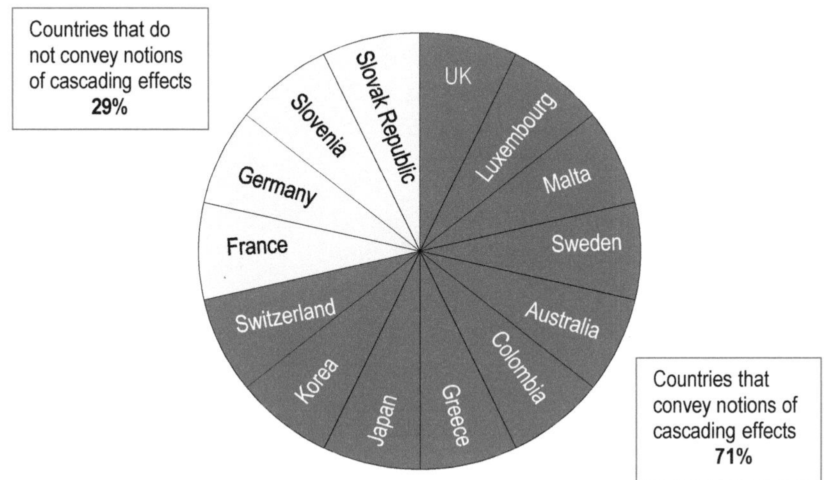

Note: Total number of responding countries: 14/19 (excluding the "don't know" and non-applicable replies).

Source: OECD Questionnaire on Risk Communication Policies and Practices. Question 2.3 (Annex A).

Figure 2.6 Communicating about known and unknown risks

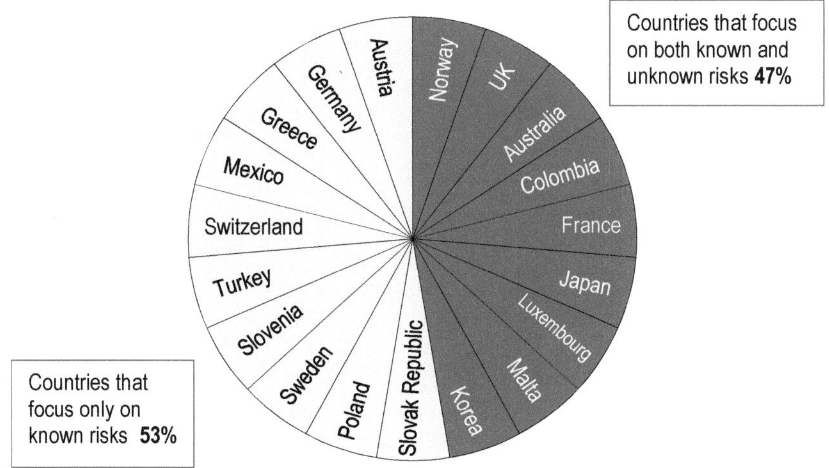

Note: Total number of responding countries: 19/19.

Source: OECD Questionnaire on Risk Communication Policies and Practices. Question 2.2 (Annex A).

Another increasingly important element of a comprehensive approach to communicating risks is the notion of trans-boundary risks. Especially major risks are increasingly expanding across administrative borders and trans-boundary risks have become an increasing challenge for national governments to address. For example, the volcanic ash cloud that formed over Iceland in 2010 highlighted the need for increased awareness of risks with the potential to affect more than one nation (Box 2.3).

Box 2.3 Transboundary risk management: the case of the Icelandic volcanic ash cloud

An eruption of the Eyjafjallajökull Volcano in 2010 in Iceland led to the development of an ash cloud that grounded 100 000 commercial and cargo airliners across Europe for several days, leaving more than 10 million passengers stranded. The estimated loss for aviation firms was EUR 2.5 billion not including the indirect damages suffered by trade relationships all around the world.

The reactive response of European transport ministries and civil aviation authorities resulted in uncertainty and delays in restarting air traffic. This came as a result of a failure to recognize in advance the potential threat presented by volcanic ash clouds from Iceland, the inflexible nature of existing aviation protocols as well as the absence of any pre-existing agreement on safe ash levels. Experts throughout Europe were confronted with a situation in which they had little understanding about the risk posed by the forming ash cloud. A precautionary approach was therefore chosen by regulators, which grounded all flights in Europe crossing the affected area.

Following Iceland's volcano eruption, European States recognised the need for a harmonised European approach on this matter. Evaluations were carried out and policy recommendations put forward highlighting the need to establish an international science panel to catalogue, evaluate and raise awareness of regional natural hazards with the potential to affect more than one nation.

Sources: WEF (2012), "New Models for Addressing Supply Chain and Transport Risk", www3.weforum.org/docs/WEF_SCT_RRN_NewModelsAddressingSupplyChainTransportRisk_Industry Agenda_2012.pdf ; ICAO (2010), *A new Era of Effective cooperation*, www.icao.int/publications/journalsreports/2010/ICAO_Reg_report_EUR-NAT_2010.pdf ; OECD (2014), *Boosting Resilience through Innovative Risk Governance*, http://dx.doi.org/10.1787/9789264209114-en.

In the OECD survey, almost all responding countries state that they integrate the notion of trans-boundary risks into their risk communication strategies (Figure 2.7). This can take the form of national institutions communicating internally about risks stemming from outside (e.g. the risk of pandemics communicated by national health offices). It can also mean formal channels to communicate about trans-boundary risks between countries, such as between Ecuador and Colombia on volcano risks or between Mexico and the United States to draw up joint contingency plans for events that could pollute shared waterways and the maritime environment.

Figure 2.7 Communicating about trans-boundary risks

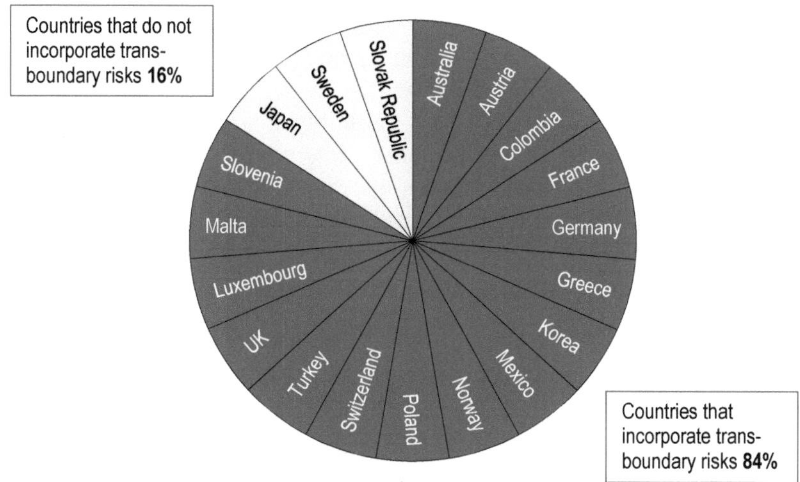

Note: Total number of responding countries: 19/19.

Source: OECD Questionnaire on Risk Communication Policies and Practices. Question 2.2 (Annex A).

Communicating about risks involves conveying complex events characterised by rapid changes and developments in the risk landscape. Therefore, risk communication needs flexible ways to deliver messages, familiarising people with the concept of uncertainty. More than two thirds of responding countries integrate the notion of uncertainty in their risk communication strategies. For example, the United Kingdom conveys uncertainty by publishing the National Risk Registers, which uses risk assessment likelihood matrices to show the probability of potential risks occurring. In Mexico, the civil protection's national communication centre conveys the notion of uncertainty using alert messages published on the official web page of the civil protection authority,[6] which highlights the probabilities of risks caused by natural phenomena occurring.

The purposes of risk communication

Risk communication can be conducted for different purposes. As discussed in Chapter 1, it is vital before hazardous events occur, to inform citizens and businesses about their potential exposure and to encourage them to invest in precautionary measures to avoid, reduce or transfer these risks. This is to be distinguished from emergency and crisis communication, which directs the recipients of a message or information toward specific actions once an event is imminent, has already begun or has just occurred.

Countries were asked to rate on a scale from 1 to 5 the purposes of their risk communications. Figure 2.8 shows the average responses in terms of importance of different purposes. It highlights that the purpose with the highest average weight in importance for countries is "raising risk awareness". Most responding countries rated "awareness raising" and "informing how to behave during hazardous events" as the most important purposes of risk communication. Encourage ex-ante measures is slightly less important than the behavioural information conveyed for actual emergency situations.

Figure 2.8 The purposes of risk communication

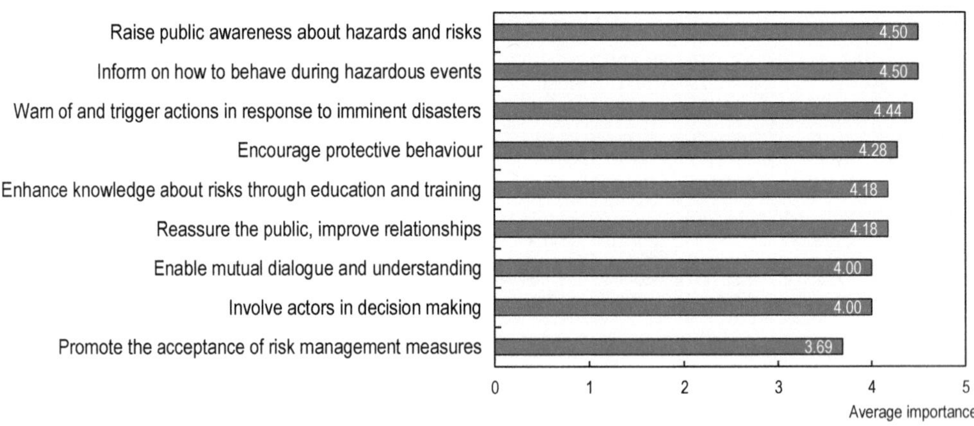

Note 1: Total number of responding countries: 18/19 (excluding non-applicable replies).
Note 2: The importance value ranges from 1 (not important) to 5 (extremely important).

Source: OECD Questionnaire on Risk Communication Policies and Practices. Question 2.5 (Annex A).

While the main focus of countries' risk communication efforts is to raise awareness of risks within countries, some have also engaged in raising global risk awareness. Japan, for example, has stressed the importance to promote a global culture of tsunami risk by proposing the "World Tsunami Awareness Day" (Box 2.4). This day will be dedicated to raise tsunami risk awareness and share innovative approaches to tsunami risk reduction.

Box 2.4 Good practice: Promoting a global culture of risk-awareness: "World Tsunami awareness day"

In the past 100 years, more than 260,000 people have perished in 58 tsunami incidents globally. At an average of 4,600 deaths per disaster, the toll has surpassed any other natural hazard. Tsunamis often cross across country boundaries, making international cooperation key to raise risk awareness and to engage in effective risk reduction measures. In recognition of the need to raise global tsunami risk awareness and international cooperation in tsunami risk reduction, in 2015 the UN General Assembly established a World Tsunami Awareness Day, to be marked each year on the 5 November. The resolution jointly proposed by 142 countries, including Japan, followed the Third UN World Conference on Disaster Risk Reduction and the 2030 Sustainable Development Agenda. Each edition of the annual day will have a thematic focus, which in 2016, for example, is about effective education and evacuation drills.

The date of 5 November was chosen in honour of an anecdote from Japan called "Inamura-no-hi", which means the "burning of the rice sheaves". During an 1854 earthquake, a farmer saw the tide receding, a sign of a looming tsunami. He set fire to his harvested rice to warn villagers, who fled to high ground. In the aftermath, he helped his community build back better to withstand future shocks, constructing an embankment and planting trees as a tsunami buffer.

Sources: UNISDR (2016), www.unisdr.org/2016/tsunamiday; Ministry of Foreign Affairs Japan (2015), Resolution on World Tsunami Awareness Day, Proposed by Japan Adopted at the Second Committee of the United Nations General Assembly (Statement by Foreign Minister Fumio Kishida), www.mofa.go.jp/press/release/press4e_000958.html.

Inclusiveness in risk communication is rated relatively lower, with the lowest importance placed on "involving actors in decision making" or "enabling mutual dialogue and understanding". These results indicate that risk communication may still be viewed traditionally, as a way to inform people about imminent threats and responses, rather than also being a holistic, long-term process which grounds risk communication more firmly in education and as a tool to promote acceptance of risk management measures, for example. This result may also suggest why many countries deem their risk communications to be ineffective. The direct involvement of all stakeholders is crucial to developing a shared understanding of complex issues that are more or less well understood by experts, but perceived very differently by the potentially affected population. A good practice example of how inclusiveness can be promoted can be seen in the cross-border initiative "Freude am Fluss" (Box 2.5).

Box 2.5 Good practice: Transboundary risk communication: Freude am Fluss (Netherlands, France, Germany)

The European-funded and Dutch-led cross-country Freude am Fluss project brought together government authorities, river managers, and natural and social scientists from the Netherlands, France and Germany to think of innovative ways to use risk communication to reduce opposition from local stakeholders against the expansion of flood plains. The project, which took place over the period 2003-2008, aimed at converting a local "not in my backyard (NIMBY) problem into a "please in my backyard" (PIMBY) opportunity, underlining the cultural and economic benefits rivers can offer. The project's objective was to:

- Develop a sustainable approach to floodplain management, recognising the limits to interfering with the natural flow and function of rivers by heightening, widening and reinforcing dykes to protect economic interests along rivers. Instead, the project aims to live with the water rather than fighting it and builds on two objectives: using technical innovations that enable the river to co-exist with land use and to enhance local creativity and entrepreneurship to realise tailor-made solutions for innovative land use.
- Develop a joint planning approach, involving various stakeholders in the planning process to create room for both the river and local interests (such as the local economy, nature and culture). This approach aims at fostering direct democracy, thereby also reducing fears and resistance of stakeholders by involving them in the process.
- Sharing lessons from the above exercises to inform actual flood management planning processes across the countries involved, especially in regional and local spatial planning.

Source: Freude am Fluss (2007), *Freude am Fluss: An Innovative Approach to River Management*, www.levenmetwater.nl/static/media/files/freudeamfluss.pdf.

Communicating about risk prevention

Although Figure 2.8 shows a relatively lower importance given by countries to the purpose of risk communication being to inform about preventative actions, when asked precisely about the prevention focus it turns out that almost all respondent countries include some information about preventative[7] measures in their risk communication strategies, and over half of them communicate extensively about preventative actions citizens can take (Figure 2.9).

Figure 2.9 Prevention focus in communicating risks

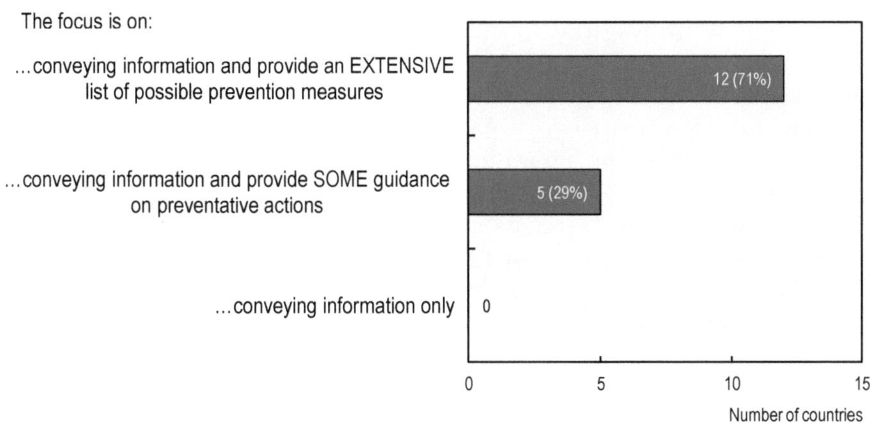

Note: Total number of responding countries: 17/19 (excluding non-applicable replies).

Source: OECD Questionnaire on Risk Communication Policies and Practices. Question 2.10 (Annex A).

In general, countries use online information portals to convey information about concrete preventative actions. For example, Greece's General Secretariat for Civil Protection issues self-protection guidelines translated into six languages on an online information portal[8] on how to prevent and mitigate the impacts of natural as well as man-made hazards. These guidelines include a list of indoor and outdoor precautionary measures that citizens should take to prevent potential damage to their properties. Similarly, France developed a new information website to inform about actions citizens should take in terms of prevention or mitigation measures, covering both natural and man-made hazards. This website conveys information about risks' exposure for all French counties and is directly linked to the Prime Minister's web site.[9] Alertswiss[10] is a Swiss example of an online platform giving information about preventive measures and the behaviour to adopt in case of disasters and emergency situations.

More traditional channels, such as brochures or written communication, are also in widespread use. For example, in Austria the authorities in charge of risk prevention use brochures to enhance knowledge about what citizens can do to protect themselves against risks. They provide brochures to home owners with a list of preventative actions they can take to protect their properties (OECD, forthcoming).

Another effective way to convey messages about the prevention of future hazards is to use markers to signal areas that have experienced disasters in the past. Some countries set up "silent witnesses" marking the location or some feature of a past disaster. Other countries use modern technology to determine hazard locations and issue warnings. For example, Australia's Emergency Alert platform (www.emergencyalert.gov.au) uses geospatial information to locate disasters and communicate warnings, which are in turn linked to applications on mobile devices.

Inclusive risk communication

As above-mentioned, to communicate effectively it is important to include all important stakeholders in the communication process. This includes citizens as much as the private sector and other interest groups, such as experts and academic institutions. Previous sections discussed the formal roles between government authorities and the private sector in the risk communication process. This section looks at the roles of a whole range of different stakeholders in the risk communication process. Figure 2.10 demonstrates that the great majority of countries involve the private sector in communicating risks in an informal way. Academic researchers are involved in about two thirds respondent countries. However, the involvement of citizens and NGOs could be strengthened, as only half of the responding countries involve them in their risk communication process.

Figure 2.10 Informal stakeholder engagement in the risk communication process

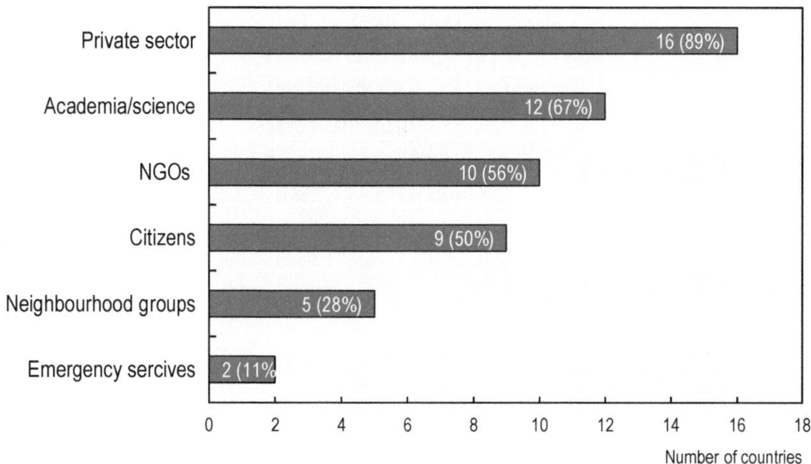

Note: Total number of responding countries: 18/19 (excluding non-applicable replies).

Source: OECD Questionnaire on Risk Communication Policies and Practices. Question 2.6.1 (Annex A).

Informal stakeholder involvement in the risk communication process takes place in many different ways. In Turkey, satellite, radio and mobile communication providers take up the role of assigning mobile base stations to areas where risks have been evaluated. In Greece, NGOs are primarily responsible for delivering the risk information provided by public authorities to citizens. In Japan, opinions from citizens, neighbourhood groups and academia are reflected in the legislation process for the development of risk communication programmes. In Australia, private telecommunication carriers disseminate emergency warning messages and NGOs such as Green Cross Australia are in charge of important risk communication websites, such as Queensland's Harden Up initiative (Box 2.6). In the United Kingdom, academic experts often work collaboratively with the UK government as spokespersons to better communicate with the general public.

Box 2.6 Good practice: Multi-stakeholder risk awareness initiative: Harden Up – Protecting Queensland Initiative (Australia)

Harden Up is a multi-stakeholder risk awareness initiative in Queensland (Australia) led by Green Cross Australia, an Australian environmental NGO helping citizens adapt to climate change. It brings together businesses, research, community and government partners to provide a state-wide online portal informing citizens about their individual vulnerability to natural hazards as well as the measures they can take to become more resilient. The practice was initiated by a Queensland government official that sought to collaborate with Green Cross Australia to build climate resilience among the state's communities. The portal is based on up-to-date climate data with the following main objectives:

- to inform citizens about their personal exposure to risks from cyclone, bushfire, severe storm and storm surge
- to inform citizens about practical actions they can take to reduce hazard exposure, such as preparing an emergency kit and instructions how to store it, having adequate insurance or clearing one's home, gutters and downpipes
- to encourage and inform about ways to engage in community resilience initiatives such as the Queensland State Emergency Service which trains volunteers to provide various support functions in emergencies
- to encourage and inform about the adoption of sustainable practices, especially by making green choices during the recovery phase of a disaster.

Besides these main objectives the portal also targets children to learn about climate change. It encourages young people to use their creativity to envisage a greener future by creating age-specific climate change learning pages and games and providing ideas and resources for teachers to use in their classrooms.

Results and impact?

Since its creation in 2011, 35 500 people have accessed the website, viewing 155 000 pages and taking 18 000 discrete actions to prepare for extreme weather events.

Potential for policy transfer?

There are ongoing discussions in Australia over broadening the scope of the website to other states. Given these initial experiences it seems this is a good practice transferable to other OECD countries as well.

Source: Green Cross Australia (2013), *Harden Up Protecting Queensland*, Commonwealth of Australia, www.nccarf.edu.au/localgov/sites/nccarf.edu.au.localgov/files/casestudies/pdf/Case%20Study_Green%20Cross%20Australia_Harden%20Up%20Protecting%20Queensland.pdf

Different groups of populations have different needs that have to be taken into account if risk communication is to be effective. For example, elderly people may have physical constraints to reacting to and adapting their behaviour to imminent emergencies. School children need to be communicated to in a different way than adults.

Looking at countries' practices, they have made significant efforts to tailor risk communication to specific vulnerable groups. Almost all responding countries pay explicit attention to vulnerable groups in communicating about risks. For example, Greece translates risk information into different languages and designs specific communication strategies to inform specific groups, such as tourists. Norway has created fire hazard communication strategies targeting elderly and disabled people. In Turkey, the Prime Ministry's Disaster and Emergency Management Authority developed a mobile phone application to inform all citizens, especially visually impaired people, about past and imminent earthquake events.[11] Having learnt from the heatwave in 2003, French authorities now pay special attention to targeting communications about heatwaves to vulnerable groups such as children and the elderly. The Ministry of Health in France provides risk communication materials online that can be used by any group engaged in risk communication efforts to communicate to specific target groups.[12] Austria's Civil Protection Association (*Zivilschutzverband*) organises competitive events at schools to raise children's risk awareness and enhance their preparedness. For example, it has held the Children's Safety Olympics every year since 2000 to teach children how to behave in emergency situations and how to avoid dangers in daily life.[13]

Finally, risk communication messages need to be tailored to specific local populations. There are several good examples of local authorities conducting more tailored messaging, The United Kingdom's Met Office conducts specific campaigns for particular areas to take into account local prevailing conditions, such as the "Ready for Winter?" campaign developed to help people living in areas vulnerable to cold weather conditions. In France, the local community information document described in Box 2.7 is an effort to raise awareness of local prevailing conditions at the municipal level across France. In Japan, municipalities are obliged to disseminate hazard maps to the public that also indicate evacuation routes to be taken and anticipated safe meeting points. In many municipalities, these maps are established in a participatory process (OECD, 2009). Since 2009, Mexican primary school programmes have integrated risk management in their curricula in history, ethics, Spanish, natural sciences, mathematics and geography. Furthermore, free books are distributed that include prevention information to each level of the primary education cycle (OECD, 2013).

Box 2.7 Good practice: Local community information document about major prevailing risks (France)

France introduced the *document d'information communal sur les risques majeurs (*DICRIM) in 1990, obliging every community, under the responsibility of the mayor and his municipal council, to draw up an information document about the safety measures to take in the event of a potential threat. The document is tailored to the locally prevailing hazards and includes information on:

- locally prevailing natural and technological risks
- measures taken by the municipality to reduce risk exposure
- safety measures to be taken in the event of an emergency or an alarm (for example behavioural measures, securing assets from areas at risk, mounting electricity and gas counters above a potential flooding level)
- a list of critical public infrastructures (including retirement homes, schools etc.)
- how land owners and those renting premises have to communicate about the safety measures stipulated in the DICRIM.

The objective of the DICRIM is to raise awareness among citizens about local major risks which they could be exposed to. The DICRIM should inform them about the nature of the threats, their potential consequences and the measures they can take to protect themselves or reduce their exposure and potential damages. The DICRIM recognises that local administrative boundaries may not be the right scale for analysing hazards and encourages inter-municipal hazard analysis, on which local prescriptions can be based.

Source: Prim.net (2009), "Le document d'information communal sur les risques majeurs (DICRIM)", www.risquesmajeurs.fr/le-document-d%E2%80%99information-communal-sur-les-risques-majeurs-dicrim (accessed September 2015).

Channels and modes of risk communication

Risk managers have a wide range of channels they can use to communicate risks. These channels can range from more traditional TV, radio or newspaper ads to information campaigns using several communication channels simultaneously. Figure 2.11 shows that the main channels are used with similar frequency across responding countries. However, only half of the countries actively use political leadership for risk communication. Germany and Colombia also deliver information through the civic code.

Figure 2.11 Channels for communicating risks

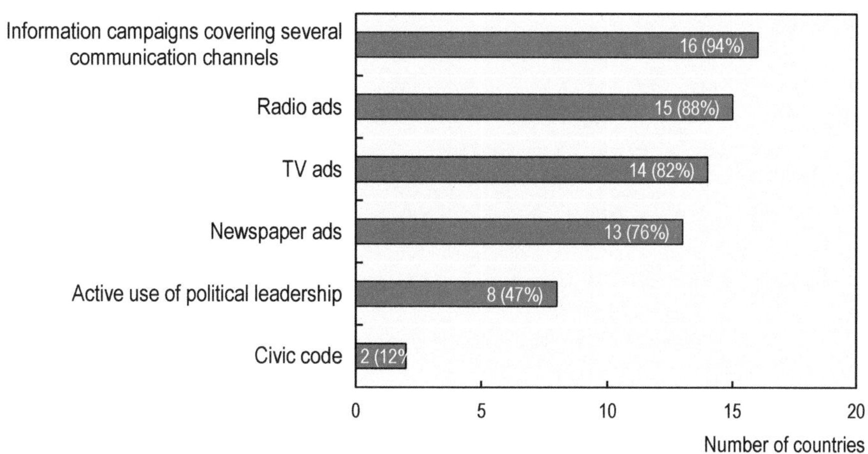

Note: Total number of responding countries: 17/19 (excluding non-applicable replies).

Source: OECD Questionnaire on Risk Communication Policies and Practices. Question 2.11 (Annex A).

The mode describes the way in which messages are delivered through each different channel. Figure 2.12 shows the use of different modes of risk communication across respondent countries. All countries deliver risk communication messages through written messages such as newspapers, letters or public advertisements. Non-verbal or visual modes of risk communication are used relatively less often.

Figure 2.12 Modes of risk communication

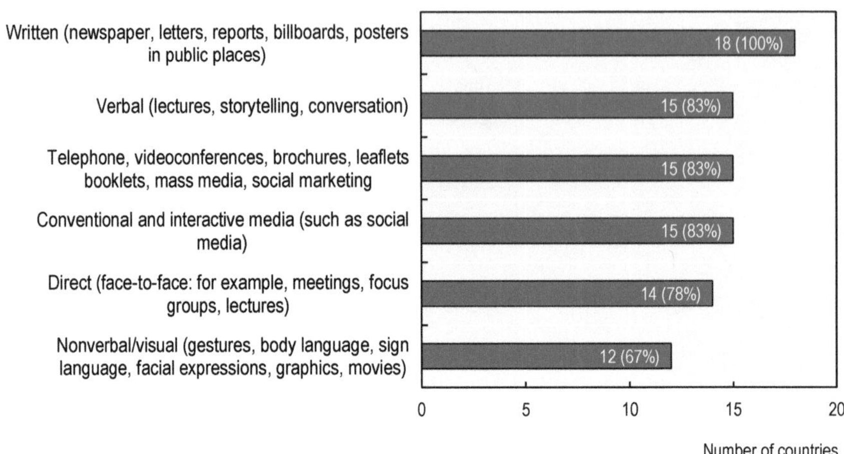

Note: Total number of responding countries: 18/19 (excluding non-applicable replies).

Source: OECD Questionnaire on Risk Communication Policies and Practices. Question 2.12 (Annex A).

The evolving role of technology for two-way communication

Relationships between message providers and message receivers based on two-way communication are the foundation of an effective risk communication. It is difficult for governments to build trust or credibility simply with one-way transfers of information. Two-way communication allows unique local characteristics and different types of communities and stakeholders to be taken into account.

Social media have become important channels and modes in effectively communicating risks. Contrary to more traditional channels of risk communication, they provide for an interactive platform, where message providers and receivers can engage in a two-way communication process. All responding countries use interactive media to communicate risks. Most of them use either Facebook or Twitter,[14] and some of them, for example Greece and Switzerland, also upload risk communication videos to YouTube,[15] or images on Instagram and Flickr.

The majority of respondent countries offer ways for citizens to provide feedback or to engage in two-way, interactive communication about risks between citizens and the government (Figure 2.13). Many countries, such as France, Norway and Switzerland, use social media to provide feedback and interactions. Similarly, in Turkey an electronic system allows citizens to reach the authorities via the Internet. For example, Korea's emergency services and police promote information sharing to precisely collect disaster information on hazard locations and disseminate alarm messages (OECD, 2015) (Box 2.8). Box 2.9 describes an example from Germany of an effective way to involve citizens and other flood risk management actors in risk communication and decision-making processes.

Figure 2.13 Interaction mechanisms from citizens to government

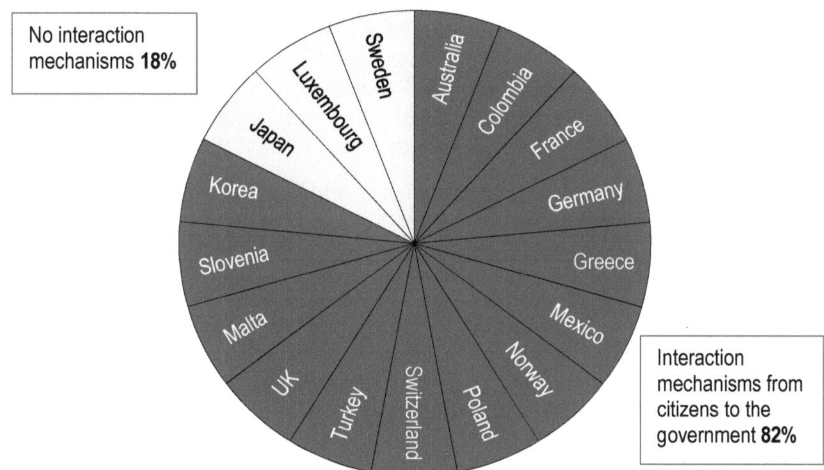

Note: Total number of responding countries: 17/19.

Source: OECD Questionnaire on Risk Communication Policies and Practices. Question 2.13 (Annex A).

Box 2.8 Good practice: Fostering information sharing: The Korean Integrated Situation Centre

The Korean Integrated Situation Center (ISC) collects, monitors and disseminates real time disaster information on a 24-hour, 365-days basis. Information is collected from 34 affiliated organisations such as the Meteorological Administration, the Flood Control Centre, local authorities, the Media and citizens, which feed in the Disaster Information Sharing System. Citizens, via either internet or telephone, feed the ISC with information on disaster impacts on the ground. In turn, the ISC analyses information and disseminates alert messages for public evacuations and disaster response to the media and the general public through the use of cell broadcasting messages.

Source: Kang, S.J. (2012), "Integrated situation management in Korea", www.oecd.org/governance/risk/korea.ppt

Box 2.9 Good practice: Integrative Flood Risk Governance Approach for Improvement of Risk Awareness and Increased Public Participation (Germany)

The Integrative Flood Risk Governance Approach for Improvement of Risk Awareness and Increased Public Participation was a project, carried out between 2009 and 2011, that looked at effective ways to involve citizens and other flood risk management actors in planning and decision-making processes with a view to improve risk communication. As part of a set of European case studies in the framework of the ERA-Net CRUE programmes (a European Commission initiative to support coordination and coherence in European flood risk management research), the German case study was carried out in Leichlingen (Rhineland), which is situated in the catchment area of the Wupper.

As a first step, the project carried out a baseline survey to gather perception data among citizens and businesses (750 surveys sent out, 15% response rate) with a view to improving risk communication. Citizens and businesses were then encouraged to participate in a set of activities alongside actors in charge of flood risk management:

- An online chat via internet, the media and TV was organised to answer to concrete questions of citizens to public authorities in charge of risk management.
- A "World Café" was organised among citizens and another among pupils to discuss flood risk management in the targeted area.

Results and impact?

The survey and a follow-up workshop among all stakeholders concluded that more tangible communication was needed to not only explain hazard zones but to translate what this could mean in terms of impacts for individual houses. A second lesson was the need to improve personal advice, as opposed to just flyers and websites. Finally, it was recommended to repeat the exercises and information so as to avoid forgetting it.

Source: Fleischhauer et al. (2012), "Risiko hochwasser", *Bevölkerungsschutz: Risikokommunikation.*

Quality assurance

Grounding risk communication in scientific evidence is key to ensuring quality and accuracy in risk communication. The great majority of countries confirm that their risk communication work is grounded in scientific evidence. This includes hazard and early warning information based on up-to-date scientific modelling, but equally the systematic collection and analysis of historical data and lessons learned from past disasters. The UK scientific advisory group is a good example of how scientific expertise can help develop effective risk communication strategies (Box 2.10).

Box 2.10 Good practice: Scientific Advisory Group in Emergencies (United Kingdom)

The UK Scientific Advisory Group in Emergencies (SAGE) is an independent support group that provides science-based expertise for the management of complex and unprecedented crises for the UK Cabinet Office. SAGE convenes in situations that require cross government co-ordination, notably when the Cabinet Office, in consultation with the Prime Minister, decides to activate the Cabinet Office Briefing Room (COBR), in response to a crisis. The SAGE provides scientific and technical advice on the development of the crisis, on potential scenarios and their impacts. Under the authority of the Government Chief Scientific Advisor, SAGE includes experts from all sectors and disciplines to analyse data, to assess existing research, or to commission new research. To inform cross-government decision-making during the emergency response and the recovery phases, the SAGE submits policy option papers which outline scientific and technical solutions. At all stages, SAGE representatives attend the COBR to explain scientific issue.

As in many OECD countries, crises affecting the UK have become more complex, with the emergence of new threats, and the evolution of several inter-connected risk factors. SAGE has been set up to meet the needs of the Cabinet Office's strategic crisis managers when confronted with complex crises.

The understanding of the complexity requires thinking across sectors, identifying potential cascading impacts and evaluating uncertainties. Having access to the best available advice in a timely fashion is key to effective crisis management decision-making. To ensure the full range of issues is considered, advice needs to stem from a range of disciplines, including the scientific, technical, economic and legal. Thus the need to set up a specific group which can quickly mobilise and peer-review multidisciplinary scientific expertise during crises.

Objectives

- To provide decision-making advice on the scientific concepts key to understanding the emergency.
- To give advice on how the emergency might develop; to outline its potential implications and evaluate related uncertainties.
- To present potential scientific solutions and options to improve assessment and monitoring.

Box 2.10 Good practice: Scientific Advisory Group in Emergencies (United Kingdom) *(continued)*

Results

- During the 2009 H1N1 influenza pandemic, SAGE informed the development of a vaccination and anti-viral strategy, the surge capacity planning, and the planning for the management of excess deaths.
- During the 2010 volcanic ash cloud, SAGE provided the scientific basis to air transport regulation measures.
- In the 2011 Great East Japan Earthquake and Fukushima nuclear accident, SAGE analysis was instrumental for the development of the public communication strategy, contingency planning, and technical briefings.

Lessons learned

- SAGE's flexibility and scalability helped to adapt to the specific nature of each disaster and its unforeseen developments.
- SAGE representatives' attendance during ministerial and official group meetings within the COBR is crucial for the explanation of scientific and technical issues to the leadership, the representative was able to present and explain the full range of SAGE views, including from specialties that are not their own.
- Peer reviews undertaken by the SAGE committee ensure the quality of advice, however if time was lacking, SAGE members relied on their own expert judgment.

*S*ource: OECD (2016), "Toolkit for risk governance", www.oecd.org/governance/toolkit-on-risk-governance/home.

Part of a good quality assurance strategy is the evaluation of the impact of risk communication polices. Such evaluations can help countries understand whether they achieved their desired objectives and, if not, what lessons can be learnt to inform future improvements in risk communication policy design. Looking at the survey results, countries could improve the long-term effectiveness of their risk communication activities through more use of evidence of their impact. Although the majority of responding countries have assessed impacts (Figure 2.14), few report any concrete results. Some countries regularly assess the levels of citizens' risk awareness, such as Austria and Sweden, but although it is very important to monitor overall awareness levels, such studies only indirectly indicate the effectiveness of specific risk communication interventions. They need to be complemented by assessment of the impact of different communication activities so to ensure their effectiveness through continuous learning in the longer run. The Loire River Basin authority in France has conducted panel business surveys to track the effectiveness of their risk communication and prevention interventions over time (Box 2.11).

Figure 2.14 Studies to assess the impact of risk communication

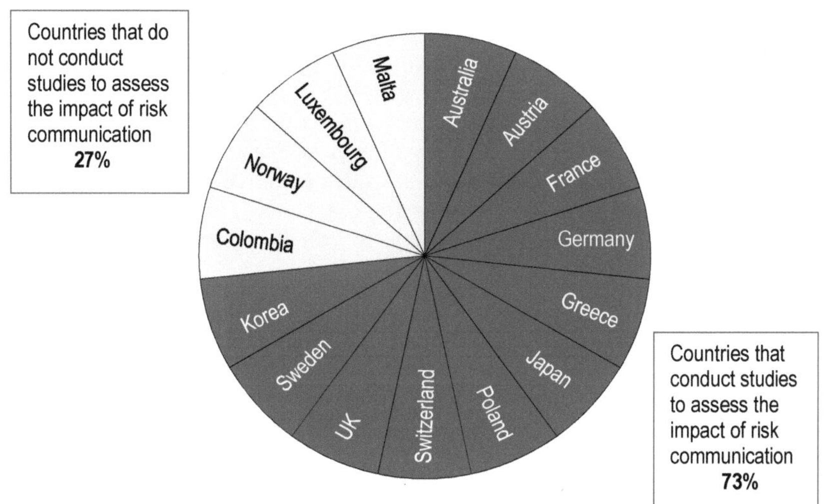

Note: Total number of responding countries: 15/19 (excluding the "don't know" and non-applicable replies).

Source: OECD Questionnaire on Risk Communication Policies and Practices. Question 3.2 (Annex A).

Box 2.11 Good practice: Tracking the effectiveness of risk awareness interventions in the Plan Loire (France)

The Plan Loire includes key activities to strengthen the risk awareness and risk reduction investments among businesses located in flood zone areas of the Loire River. To evaluate the effectiveness of their activities, the public authority in charge of implementing the measures undertook a baseline survey in 2009 to assess risk awareness before any intervention. The results of the baseline survey carried out in 2009 among 1 700 companies in the Loire River basin showed that 53% of business owners whose activity was located in a flood zone were completely unaware of their exposure.

Box 2.11 Good practice: Tracking the effectiveness of risk awareness interventions in the Plan Loire (France) *(continued)*

A follow-up survey was carried out in 2012 to evaluate the various measures to raise awareness about risk exposure, measures that reduce exposure, and opportunities to find co-financing for such measures. The public authority found that business owners who carried out a vulnerability diagnostic (provided for free for all business owners) were more aware of the flood risk danger and their individual exposure than those that did not take up this opportunity to get a free diagnostic.[1] The authorities in charge were clearly able to demonstrate that, overall, their risk communication activities were effective and by looking more closely at the results, could see what worked better and for whom. Impact evaluations like this one can crucially inform the design of future risk communication strategies.

1. For both survey waves and results, see the page "Résultats de l'enquête téléphonique 2012", on the Plan Loire website at www.plan-loire.fr/fr/les-plates-formes/prevention-des-inondations/demarche-industrielle/environnementfavorable/enquetesperceptionrisque/barometre-2012/index.html.

Source: OECD (2010), *Étude de l'OCDE sur la gestion des risques d'inondation: Bassin de la Loire, France 2010*, http://dx.doi.org/10.1787/9789264056817-en.

Training and education

Risk communication is characterised by uncertainty, with rapid change and developments in the risk landscape requiring ever more flexible and rapid ways to communicate risks. This highlights the importance of making the most of modern information technologies and carefully weighing the benefits (and potential risks) of using social media to effectively communicate about risks. For these reasons risk communication staff need to be continuously and well trained. Figure 2.15 shows that almost all responding countries update their staff through in-work training and that 67% of responding countries also use external training and self-learning materials.

Online training can be effective in improving disaster preparedness by sharing information with a larger community on the web. However, only 33% of the responding countries use this type of training. One interesting example of such training is the online application "Worst Case Hero",[16] which was adapted for use in six countries (Bulgaria, United Kingdom, France, Germany, Latvia and Romania). The application allows participants to learn about preparing for three different emergencies and then test their knowledge.

Figure 2.15 Training of risk communication staff

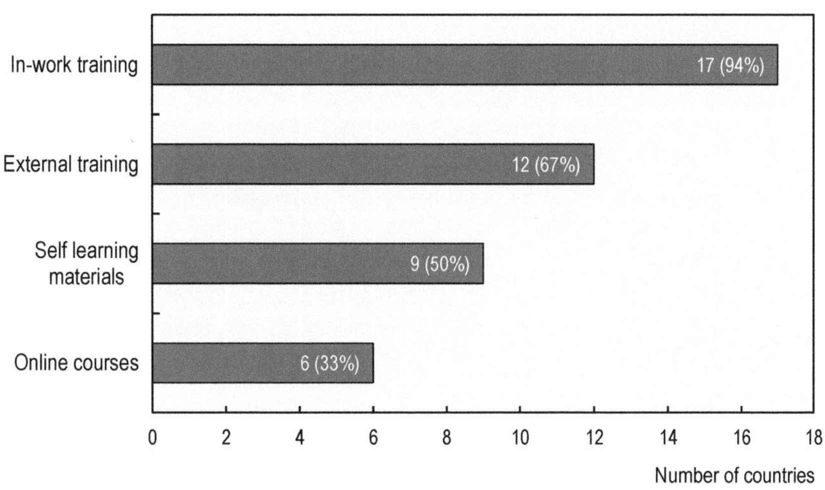

Note: Total number of responding countries: 18/19 (excluding non-applicable replies).

Source: OECD Questionnaire on Risk Communication Policies and Practices. Question 3.4 (Annex A).

Conclusions

The results of the OECD questionnaire on risk communication policies and practices presented in this chapter have highlighted good practice from several countries as well as areas where improvements to policies can be made. The next chapter provides a set of policy recommendations to support national measures for risk communication and discusses options for taking this work forward.

Notes

1. Kriseinfo website, at: www.kriseinfo.no/en.
2. Emergency Alert website, at: www.emergencyalert.gov.au.
3. See the information about the Seveso Directive at: http://ec.europa.eu/environment/seveso.
4. See for example the General Secretariat's self-protection guidelines at: http://civilprotection.gr/en/disasters.
5. See the National Risk Register of Civil Emergencies at: www.gov.uk/government/collections/national-risk-register-of-civil-emergencies.
6. Available at: www.gob.mx/segob/documentos/alertamientos-de-proteccioncivil-atiende-recomendaciones-del-sinaproc.
7. This includes organisational and structural measures people can take to reduce their risk exposure (such as reinforcing houses), but also preparedness measures such as putting an emergency kit together and being informed about behavioural measures to be taken at the onset of a disaster.
8. Self-protection guidelines, available at: http://civilprotection.gr/en/disasters.
9. Available at: www.gouvernement.fr/risques.
10. Alertswiss website, at: https://alertswiss.ch.
11. Deprem Bilgi Sistemleri (Earthquake Information Systems), at: www.afad.gov.tr/tr/HbIcerikDetay.aspx?ID=96.
12. Available at: http://inpes.santepubliquefrance.fr/10000/themes/evenement_climatique/canicule/canicule-outils.asp.
13. SAFETY-Tour Bundesfinale 2015, at: www.zivilschutzverband.at/de_at/home/194.
14. For example: Fire and Rescue NSW on Facebook (Australia): www.facebook.com/frnsw; Swissalert on Twitter (Switzerland): https://twitter.com/swissalert.

15. For example Swissalert video on YouTube: www.youtube.com/watch?v=w3IyFqk2D0Y.
16. See the Aware and Resilient project's Worst Case Hero at www.ar-project.eu/en/play/worst-case-hero/.

Bibliography

Austrian Civil Protection Association, www.zivilschutzverband.at/home.

Fleischhauer, M., S. Greiving, M. Scheibel, M. Ebers and F. Flex (2012), "Risiko hochwasser", *Bevölkerungsschutz: Risikokommunikation*, Vol. 4/2012. Bundesamt für Bevölkerungsschutz und Katastrophenhilfe, Berlin.

Freude am Fluss (2007), *Freude am Fluss: An Innovative Approach to River Management*, Living with Water, Nijmegen, www.innovatieagroennatuur.nl/downloadattachment.php?id=11_KXy8ZduTZQKqH1MffW9.

Green Cross Australia (2013), *Harden Up Protecting Queensland*, Commonwealth of Australia, https://www.nccarf.edu.au/localgov/sites/nccarf.edu.au.localgov/files/casestudies/pdf/Case%20Study_Green%20Cross%20Australia_Harden%20Up%20Protecting%20Queensland.pdf.

ICAO (2010), "Operations within areas of possible presence of volcanic ash", *A new Era of Effective cooperation*, Canada, www.icao.int/publications/journalsreports/2010/ICAO_Reg_report_EUR-NAT_2010.pdf.

Kang, S.J. (2012), "Integrated situation management in Korea", Presentation at First OECD/Swiss Federal Chancellery Workshop on Strategic Crisis Management, Geneva, Switzerland, 28 June 2012, http://www.oecd.org/governance/risk/korea.ppt.

Ministry of Foreign Affairs Japan (2015), Resolution on World Tsunami Awareness Day, Proposed by Japan Adopted at the Second Committee of the United Nations General Assembly (Statement by Foreign Minister Fumio Kishida),www.mofa.go.jp/press/release/press4e_000958.html.

Ministry of Interior, Austria (2016), Information on Austria's Civil Protection Agency, www.bmi.gv.at/cms/BMI_Zivilschutz_en/national/civil/start.aspx.

Mission Risques Naturels (2015), *Insurance and Climate Risks Prevention*, Mission Risques Naturels, www.mrn.asso.fr/system/files/15%2010%2001%20Brochure%20Prevention%20VAng.pdf.

OECD (forthcoming) "Boosting resilience through innovative risk governance: The case of alpine areas in Austria", OECD, Paris.

OECD (2016), "Toolkit for risk governance", OECD website, www.oecd.org/governance/toolkit-on-risk-governance/home.

OECD (2015), *The Changing Face of Strategic Crisis Management*, OECD Publishing, Paris, http://dx.doi.org/10.1787/9789264249127-en.

OECD (2014), *Boosting Resilience through Innovative Risk Governance*, OECD Publishing, Paris, http://dx.doi.org/10.1787/9789264209114-en.

OECD (2013), *OECD Reviews of Risk Management Policies: Mexico 2013: Review of the Mexican National Civil Protection System*, OECD Publishing, Paris, http://dx.doi.org/10.1787/9789264192294-en.

OECD (2010), *Étude de l'OCDE sur la gestion des risques d'inondation: Bassin de la Loire, France 2010*, OECD Publishing, Paris. http://dx.doi.org/10.1787/9789264056817-en

OECD (2009), *OECD Reviews of Risk Management Policies: Japan 2009: Large-Scale Floods and Earthquakes*, OECD Publishing, Paris, http://dx.doi.org/10.1787/9789264050303-en.

Prim.net (2009). "Le document d'information communal sur les risques majeurs (DICRIM)", Risques Majeurs website, www.risquesmajeurs.fr/le-document-d%E2%80%99information-communal-sur-les-risques-majeurs-dicrim (accessed September 2015).

UNISDR (2016), World Tsunami Awareness Day, http://www.unisdr.org/2016/tsunamiday.

WEF (2012), "New Models for Addressing Supply Chain and Transport Risk", World Economic Forum, Geneva, www3.weforum.org/docs/WEF_SCT_RRN_NewModelsAddressingSupplyChainTransportRisk_Industry_Agenda_2012.pdf.

Chapter 3

Recommendations for improving risk communication policies and practices

This chapter summarises the policy recommendations for improving countries' risk communication policies and practices. It highlights the importance and central role of leadership and partnerships in communicating risks effectively. It also emphasises the large untapped potential for using risk communication as a tool to boost resilience against disasters, looking beyond simply preparedness and crisis communication. The chapter concludes with recommendations for taking the present work forward, specifically drawing attention to the need for more focused, in-depth studies of country practices to follow this cross-country overview.

Policy recommendations

This report compares risk communication policies and practices across OECD countries, with a view to communicating about the prevention of risks, rather than simply preparedness or crisis communication. It uses a survey instrument derived from the policy recommendations put forward in the OECD Recommendation on the Governance of Critical Risks and the EU Council Conclusions on an Integrated Approach to more Effective Risk, Emergency and Crisis Communication.

Overall, the results of the survey point to the need of strengthening a whole-of-society approach to risk communication. **Risk communication across OECD countries could be improved by more effectively including stakeholders**, especially the private sector. To date, countries have ensured strong central leadership in risk communication, with central risk communication tasks shared with local governments. However, to increase the effectiveness of risk communication, governments could include other stakeholders better and more systematically in the communication process. **Building stronger and more systematic partnerships, especially with the private sector, could help to improve the exchange of critical risk information**. This is key, for example, in the area of critical infrastructure protection, where governments have responsibility for ensuring safety and continued service, but do not always have direct regulatory oversight of critical infrastructure services. As well as sharing information, the private sector could make important contributions towards designing effective risk communication policies and could help ensure risk communication effectively targets different stakeholder groups. Including the private sector in risk communication could also boost the engagement of businesses in ensuring business continuity and resilience of their assets and services.

An increased focus on an all-hazards approach to risk communication could overcome silo and redundant efforts in countries' risk communication efforts. The survey results show that countries have tended to communicate risks in silos. Administrative boundaries across government departments determine the risks that are addressed in their respective communication strategies, which means that risks are communicated separately from one another. To increase the effectiveness of risk communication, it is important to address multiple hazards simultaneously. This is especially important to communicate about key national risks, but also more concretely when communication is about cascading risks. Good examples of how countries can implement this in practice include Australia's Harden-Up initiative, which communicates about multiple natural hazards, their cascading impacts and ways to protect against multiple risks.

Crisis communication has been widely and well established across OECD countries, while more could be done to focus risk communication on prevention and mitigation. **Countries have established strong crisis communication policies and practices**. Countries widely recognise the importance of risk communication for crisis situations and have established solid crisis communication policies and practices. However, more countries could make risk communication also about risk prevention, informing stakeholders about what they can do to reduce their risk exposure. Responding countries have all developed tools to communicate about what potential risks exist in which part of their countries. Often, this information is conveyed in easily accessible and easy-to-use tools, where individual stakeholders can view their exact location's exposure to risk. However, this is not enough. **Countries could strengthen their efforts by communicating about the actions individual stakeholders can take to reduce their risk exposure**.

Countries also need to fully exploit new technology, including social media, which can also facilitate a two-way, interactive flow of information and address rapid developments in current risk landscapes. Traditional crisis communication has been particularly one-sided, delivering messages in a top-down approach. For risk communication to be effective, actors need to be actively in the communication process, by creating two-way flows of information. This will ensure that risk information is well received as well as improved based on citizens' needs and feedback. In addition this will help to develop a shared understanding of risks and to maintain trust in government's ability to manage risks. Information communication technologies, including social media, could be further exploited to facilitate two-way flows of information. Social media can also address rapid changes and developments in the risk landscape that require more flexible ways to communicate risks. Countries could use new technologies to issue warnings more effectively and interact with affected people during ongoing crises, although ensuring that benefits and potential risks of using social media are evaluated and managed.

Grounding risk communication in scientific evidence is key to ensure quality and accuracy in risk communication. Grounding work in scientific evidence based on up-to-date scientific modelling will help to promote new tools for a more comprehensive risk communication improving its effectiveness in the longer run.

Going forward

This report represents an important first step towards understanding countries' institutional approaches for communicating risks. The results provide a first insight into countries' strengths and potential areas of improvements with regard to their risk communication policies and practices. In the future it will be important to evaluate country practices in more detail, including the role and activities of each relevant actor, the perception of different activities by their target audiences, and the effectiveness of their risk communication efforts. In-depth country case studies can provide more practical insights. Country-based studies could shed light on the difficulties countries may face in making risk communication more inclusive, especially in exchanging important information between the government and critical infrastructure operators. Such studies could also understand current evaluation practices of risk communication activities and could propose tools and methods to increase rigorous evaluation and incorporating lessons learnt into future risk communication practices.

Annex A.

OECD Questionnaire on Risk communication policies and practices

Definitions

Critical Risks: threats and hazards that pose the most strategically significant risk, as a result of (i) their probability or likelihood and of (ii) the national significance of their disruptive consequences, including sudden onset events (e.g. earthquakes, industrial accidents, terrorist attacks), gradual onset events (e.g. pandemics), and steady-state risks (notably those related to illicit trade or organised crime).

Hazard: a natural or man-made source or cause of harm or difficulty.

---

1. General institutional arrangements for government communication about risks

Policy

1.1. What is/are the main national policy(ies) in your country that mandates and/ or guides risk communication activities across sectors and levels of government?

Please list the relevant policies, if possible briefly describe each of them and kindly attach documents (or links to available documentation online) outlining these policies.

The following questions relate to what is described in the above policies, or, in their absence, may refer to what the general practice is in your country:

Actors

1.2. Who are the main actors with legal or formal responsibility for risk communication in your country? *Check all that apply*

- ☐ National government
- ☐ Local government
- ☐ Other public agencies, if so, *please specify*___________________
- ☐ International organisations
- ☐ Scientists and experts
- ☐ Industry, private sector
- ☐ Critical infrastructure providers
- ☐ NGOs and voluntary organisations
- ☐ Media
- ☐ Other, *please specify* ___________________________

1.3. Do specific actors have specific risks that they have to communicate about (i.e. is there a determined ownership of risks by certain actors)?

- ☐ Yes
- ☐ No
- ☐ I don't know

If yes, please provide examples.

1.4. Is there a lead organisation or co-ordinating platform for risk communication?

- ☐ Yes
- ☐ No
- ☐ I don't know

If yes, please provide name and describe briefly.

Private Sector

1.5. Does the private sector have any formal responsibility for risk communication?

- ☐ Yes
- ☐ No

☐ I don't know

If yes, please describe the private sector formal role and perhaps actual activities.

1.6. Are there any examples of private sector actors not living up to their legal or formal responsibilities with regard to risk communication?

☐ Yes
☐ No
☐ I don't know

If yes, please specify examples or instances where this has been the case.

1.7. What are the key processes for exchanging information about risks between government institutions and major private sector organisations? *Check all that apply*

☐ Periodic meetings (with a fixed schedule)
☐ Spontaneous meetings (called upon specific needs)
☐ Informal channels (telephone, email)
☐ Written reports available periodically
☐ Written reports available eventually
☐ Other, *please specify* ___________________________

2. Design of risk communication activities

Risk Types

2.1. Is there an all-hazard approach to risk communication or is risk communication exclusively conducted for specific hazards?

☐ It is exclusively conducted for specific hazards
☐ An all-hazards approach to risk communication is in place
☐ I don't know

Please provide examples, to illustrate the all-hazard or single hazard approaches to communicating about risks.

2.2. What is the focus of the risk communication strategies in terms of known/experienced risks or unknown/not yet experienced risks?

☐ The focus is exclusively on known/experienced risks

☐ The focus is on both experienced and unknown/not yet experienced risks

Please provide examples, if possible.

2.3. Are notions of complexity and cascading effects conveyed in risk communication?

☐ Yes

☐ No

☐ I don't know

If yes, please provide examples of how those notions are conveyed in risk communication.

2.4. Does risk communication incorporate trans-boundary risks?

☐ Yes

☐ No

☐ I don't know

If yes, please provide examples of how these notions of trans-boundary risks are conveyed in risk communication.

Purposes

2.5. Generally speaking what would you say are the purposes of risk communication in your country?

Check all that apply or please assign an importance value to each of the below items in your work from 1 (not important) to 5(extremely important).

☐ Raise public awareness about hazards and risks
☐ Enhance knowledge about risks through education and training
☐ Encourage protective behaviour
☐ Promote the acceptance of risk management measures
☐ Inform on how to behave during hazardous events
☐ Warn of and trigger actions in response to imminent and current events
☐ Reassure the public, improve relationships (build trust, cooperation, networks)
☐ Enable mutual dialogue and understanding
☐ Involve actors in decision making
☐ Other, *please specify* ____________________________

Stakeholder engagement

2.6. Are stakeholders from the private sector or NGOs or citizens involved in the design process of risk communication?

☐ Yes
☐ No
☐ I don't know

If yes:

2.6.1. Which of the following stakeholders are involved in framing the communication processes? *Check all that apply*

☐ NGOs
☐ Private sector
☐ Academia
☐ Neighbourhood groups
☐ Citizens
☐ Other, *please specify* ____________________________

2.7. Are stakeholders involved in the actual communication process?

☐ Yes
☐ No

☐ I don't know

If yes, please provide examples.

2.8. Does risk communication policy include a specific focus on vulnerable population groups (e.g. elderly/youth, disabled, linguistic minorities)?

☐ Yes
☐ No
☐ I don't know

If yes, please provide examples.

Prevention-focused risk communication

2.9. Does risk communication include communication about actions citizens should take in terms of prevention or mitigation measures?

☐ Yes
☐ No
☐ I don't know

If yes, please provide examples.

2.10. Is the focus of the type of risk communication you are in charge of on conveying information about risks, or does it emphasize information about actions citizens could take to prevent/ mitigate risks?

Please, indicate approximately on the scale provided below.

Convey information	Convey information and provide some guidance on preventative actions	Convey information and provide an extensive list of possible prevention measures
1☐	2☐	3☐

If needed, you may comment on your assessment here:

Modes and channels of risk communication

2.11. What are the channels through which risk communication is delivered? *Check all that apply*

- ☐ TV ads
- ☐ Radio ads
- ☐ Newspapers ads
- ☐ Information campaigns covering several communication channels
- ☐ Active use of political leadership
- ☐ Other, *please specify*______________________________

2.12. What are the modes that are used in the above channels for communicating? *Check all that apply*

- ☐ Written (newspaper, letters, reports, billboards, posters in public places)
- ☐ Verbal (lectures, storytelling, conversation)
- ☐ Non-verbal/visual (gestures, body language, sign language, facial expressions, graphics, movies)
- ☐ Direct (face-to-face: for example, meetings, focus groups, lectures)
- ☐ Telephone, videoconferences or if larger audience, brochures, leaflets booklets mass media and social marketing
- ☐ Conventional and interactive media (such as social media) information networks
- ☐ Other, *please specify* ______________________________

2.13. Are there feedback or interaction mechanisms from citizens to the governments?

- ☐ Yes
- ☐ No
- ☐ I don't know

Please, describe how such feedback and interaction is taking place.

2.14. Is interactive media (such as social networks) used to communicate about risks?

If yes:

2.14.1. What type of social networks do you use:

- ☐ Twitter
- ☐ Facebook

☐ Instagram
☐ Others, *please specify*______________________________

Please, provide examples on the use of social media

Tools

2.15. What kinds of tools are used to communicate?

☐ Signs marking the location of features of a past disaster (e.g. marking historical disaster events in a visible way)
☐ Maps that indicate the geographic extent of past hazardous events
☐ Other, *please specify*______________________________

2.16. How are modern technologies used to enhance risk communication (such as satellite-based technologies and systems utilising space-driven geospatial information), including mobile based content and apps? *Please provide examples.*

2.17. How has behavioural science been used to improve the effectiveness of risk communication? What results of psychological experiments have been informative to the design of risk communication practices? *Please provide examples, if possible.*

Message – framing of communication messages

2.18. Does risk communication include communicating about uncertainty?

☐ Yes
☐ No
☐ I don't know

If yes, please provide examples.

2.19. Are messages and language adapted to different recipients of the communication?

☐ Yes
☐ No
☐ I don't know

If yes, please provide examples.

2.20. Are prevailing conditions in various areas of the country taken into account?

☐ Yes
☐ No
☐ I don't know

If yes, please provide examples.

3. Good governance arrangements

Risk communication based on good governance

3.1. Are measures in place to ensure that risk communication is grounded in (scientific) evidence?

☐ Yes
☐ No
☐ I don't know

If yes, please provide examples.

Impact of risk communication

3.2. Are there any studies to assess the impact of risk communication in your country?

☐ Yes
☐ No
☐ I don't know

If yes, please describe the results and if possible attach any available documentation.

[ ]

3.3. Is there an integrated approach to risk, crisis and emergency communication?

☐ Yes
☐ No
☐ I don't know

If yes, is the integrated approach stipulated in a law or a guidance document provided by national or international agencies. Please provide relevant documentation.

[ ]

Training of risk communication staff

3.4. How is training and education of staff dealing with risk communication ensured and organised?

☐ Online courses
☐ In-work training
☐ External training
☐ Self-learning materials
☐ Other, *please specify*: ________________________________

If you would like to add a description of the training activities you engage in, please provide it here:

[ ]

If there is anything you want to add to the questionnaire that you deem important to the subject but not sufficiently covered, please feel free to add it here and/or send us any additional information through e-mail: *Cathérine Gamper (Catherine.gamper@oecd.org ; +33 1 45 24 96 11).*

[ ]

Annex B.

List of responding countries and responding institutions

Country	Name of the ministry/department or organisation
Australia 1	Government of South Australia – South Australian Fire and Emergency Services Commission
Australia 2	Australian Government - Attorney-General's Department
Austria	Ministry of the Interior
Colombia	Republic Presidency - National Unit for Disaster Risk Management (UNGRD)
France 1	Prime Minister – General Secretariat for Defence and National Security
France 2	Ministry of Interior – International Relations Mission
Germany	Documents from Germany inserted by the OECD Secretariat
Greece	Ministry of Interior - General Secretariat for Civil Protection (GSCP)
Japan	Ministry of Land, Infrastructure, Transport and Tourism (MLIT)
Korea	Ministry of Public Safety and Security- National Disaster Management Institute
Luxembourg	Ministry of State / High-Commissioner for national security
Malta	Civil Protection Department
Mexico	Ministry of the Interior – Directorate-General for Civil Protection
Norway	Ministry of Justice and Public Security
Poland	Government Centre for Security
Slovak Republic	Ministry of Interior - Department of Crisis Management
Slovenia	Administration of the Republic of Slovenia for Civil Protection and Disaster Relief, MoD
Sweden	Swedish Civil Contingencies Agency (MSB)
Switzerland	Federal Office of Civil Protection
Turkey	Prime Minister – Disaster and Emergency Management Presidency (AFAD)
United Kingdom	Cabinet Office (CO), Civil Contingencies Secretariat (CCS)

ORGANISATION FOR ECONOMIC CO-OPERATION AND DEVELOPMENT

The OECD is a unique forum where governments work together to address the economic, social and environmental challenges of globalisation. The OECD is also at the forefront of efforts to understand and to help governments respond to new developments and concerns, such as corporate governance, the information economy and the challenges of an ageing population. The Organisation provides a setting where governments can compare policy experiences, seek answers to common problems, identify good practice and work to co-ordinate domestic and international policies.

The OECD member countries are: Australia, Austria, Belgium, Canada, Chile, the Czech Republic, Denmark, Estonia, Finland, France, Germany, Greece, Hungary, Iceland, Ireland, Israel, Italy, Japan, Korea, Latvia, Luxembourg, Mexico, the Netherlands, New Zealand, Norway, Poland, Portugal, the Slovak Republic, Slovenia, Spain, Sweden, Switzerland, Turkey, the United Kingdom and the United States. The European Union takes part in the work of the OECD.

OECD Publishing disseminates widely the results of the Organisation's statistics gathering and research on economic, social and environmental issues, as well as the conventions, guidelines and standards agreed by its members.

OECD PUBLISHING, 2, rue André-Pascal, 75775 PARIS CEDEX 16
(42 2016 25 1 P) ISBN 978-92-64-26040-5 – 2016

www.ingramcontent.com/pod-product-compliance
Lightning Source LLC
LaVergne TN
LVHW070217110826
845147LV00003B/593